Adapting to Conditions

✳ OUTSTANDING ON
BRITISH ADAPTATION
TO WILDERNESS
WARFARE IN 7 YRS WAR
IN NORTH AMERICA

Adapting

to

Conditions

WAR AND SOCIETY
IN THE
EIGHTEENTH
CENTURY

EDITED BY MAARTEN ULTEE

The University of Alabama Press

LIBRARY OF CONGRESS CATALOGING IN PUBLICATION DATA

Main entry under title:

Adapting to conditions.

Includes index.
1. Military history, Modern—18th century—Congresses.
2. Sociology, Military—History—18th century—Congresses.
I. Ultee, Maarten, 1949–
U39.A327 1986   355'.009'033   85–993
ISBN 0–8173–0267–0

Contents

Acknowledgments

In submitting this volume to the press and the public, the editor has benefited greatly from the support and advice of various friends. In particular I wish to thank the cochairman of the tenth Wilburt S. Brown Conference in History, Professor Robert Erwin Johnson, whose gentlemanly counsel was invaluable in the planning and execution of this work. Professor William D. Barnard, the enterprising Chairman of the Department of History of The University of Alabama, has had a large share in reviving the Wilburt S. Brown conferences, making them a regular feature of intellectual life at the university. Professor Barnard was also instrumental in obtaining the welcome support of Douglas E. Jones, Dean of the College of Arts and Sciences, and of Dr. Roger Sayers, Academic Vice-President of the university. General Wilburt S. Brown, whose name the conference bears, had a distinguished career in the United States Marine Corps before studying and teaching at the university until his death in 1968. The capable secretaries of the Department of History, Ruth Kibbey and Kitty Sassaman, performed magnificently before, during, and after the conference. At an early stage, Malcolm M. MacDonald, Director of The University of Alabama Press, agreed to read the manuscript; later he secured helpful critical comments from two outside readers. I am also grateful for the support and suggestions provided by colleagues at Maxwell Air Force Base, especially Major Earl H. Tilford, Jr., and my officer-students there, who have helped me to refine my ideas of military history. Throughout my historical work over more than a decade, William Ritchey Newton of New York City has placed his friendly critical encouragement at my disposal; I thank him again now. My family and Mr. and Mrs. C. R. Wyatt showed interest in this work as well. For valuable editorial help I am indebted to the staff of The University of Alabama Press, and for inspiration to Sarah Bevan. Finally, I am happy to note that the editing and writing were completed in the wonderful facilities of the Herzog August Bibliothek, Wolfenbüttel, whose Director, Professor Dr. Paul Raabe, and staff warmly welcomed a wandering scholar.

Adapting to Conditions

Adapting to
Conditions

MAARTEN ULTEE

With typical short-sightedness and pride, the twentieth century has hastily claimed for itself the dubious honor of having invented "total war." Yet the study of earlier ages reminds us that war, even total war, has been a persistent plague on humanity. The paradoxes of eighteenth-century warfare, for example, are no more strange than our own. In that age wars ostensibly fought with aristocratic honor ruined once-great families, produced fortunes for upstart adventurers, and caused unspeakable horror for the civilian population. Conflicts that began with petty greed in Europe often spread throughout the globe, wherever civilized Europeans had brought their beneficent rule. Struggles for independence and human rights retained some forms of oppression and introduced still others. The peaceful images of eighteenth-century English noblemen and women in portraits by Gainsborough and Reynolds, the beauty and order of formal gardens at Versailles and Herrenhausen, the exquisite harmonies of classical music by Bach, Handel, Haydn, and Mozart—all belie a violent age. On the European continent the great powers and lordly patrons of culture were officially at war for well over half the years of the century, and their record is only marginally better than that of their sixteenth- and seventeenth-century predecessors.

1

Despite the pacific intentions of ministers such as Sir Robert Walpole and Cardinal Fleury, questions of empire and succession loomed most prominently among the causes of these wars. No self-respecting European government could ignore the dangers to international order caused by shifts in the balance of power, which was supposed to keep the peace. It was sometimes necessary to make war in order to have peace, and our ancestors were not unaware of this paradox as they celebrated their grand victories with fireworks, fountains, and the high mass *Te Deum*. They mourned their heavy losses more quietly, and they attended peace conferences to redraw the maps of Europe and the colonial world. Total war, requiring years of sacrifice from every subject as combatant, civilian living in a war zone, or taxpayer was well known in the eighteenth century.

Of course, early modern rulers did not possess the systems of rapid communication and transport that have so changed the nature of contemporary warfare. It might take weeks for diplomats in Europe to communicate with their home governments; news of an incident in the colonies in America or Asia might take months to reach London or Paris. Finally, *doing* anything military required a season or more. Organizing expeditions across the North Sea or from Rhine to Danube took time, as ships, horses, guns, and men had to be assembled and concentrated when the weather was favorable and the budget permitted. Public opinion was perhaps less of a concern for eighteenth-century monarchs, enlightened or not, than for republican governments. But historians have observed official attempts to manage the news in an age when information was much more costly than it is now. There were, for example, propagandistic appeals to growing national consciousness. This consciousness in the form of passionate hatreds between ordinary people of neighboring states at times ran far ahead of official policy. Indeed, it was useful: once ministers had met with sovereigns in their councils and taken decisions about the war, lawyers and pamphleteers played their part in arousing enthusiasm for the war effort. But the important decisions were made by command—funds were found, diverted, borrowed or extracted from the people; armies and fleets were recruited, supplied, and dispatched slowly to do their duty. Time and space may have limited the possibilities in eighteenth-century warfare, but one does not have to be a militarist or enthusiast for war to recognize its historical importance despite those limitations. Whether we agree with Werner Sombart that war is the source of technological progress, or with Voltaire that it is the greatest expression of greed, ambition, and inhumanity, we have difficulty imagining history without it.[1] Indeed, Herodotus and Thucydides, the ancient founders of serious historical study, regarded war as the greatest of subjects, the most worthy of learned investigation and permanent record. Their medieval and Renaissance successors generally shared this opinion, whether their subjects were the struggles of the Merovingians, the Italian city-states, or Protestants and Catholics during the Reformation. "The story of the human race is war," declared Winston Churchill, whose talents as historian were evident well before his gifts as a wartime leader.[2]

The best historians did not limit themselves to laconic chronicles of battles but rather considered the causes of conflicts, their effects on the rise and decline of rulers and nations. Nor did they consider war in abstraction, apart from other human institutions. Because human beings so often resorted to war, it was a social problem requiring general explanations. By the seventeenth century Hugo Grotius had defined war as "the state of those who attempt to settle their differences by means of force."[3] Grotius suggested that some generally accepted laws were necessary to civilize it. His contempo-

[1]Werner Sombart, *Krieg und Kapitalismus*, vol. 2 of *Studien zur Entwicklungsgeschichte des modernen Kapitalismus* (Munich: Duncker and Humblot, 1913). "Surely it is a very fine art which leaves the countryside desolate, destroys houses, and in a typical year causes 40,000 of every 100,000 men to perish." Voltaire, "Guerre," *Dictionnaire philosophique portatif* (London, n.p. [Geneva: Cramer], 1764), p. 197.
[2]Quoted by Asa Briggs, *A Social History of England* (London: Weidenfeld and Nicolson, 1983), p. 250.
[3]Hugo Grotius, "Belli definitio et origo nominis, Quid bellum, quid jus?" *De Jure Belli et Pacis* (Paris: N. Buon, 1625), bk. 1, chap. 1, II, p. 2.

rary Thomas Hobbes postulated the state of war as the aboriginal state of nature—the fearful struggle of all against all, restrained in civil society only by a powerful sovereign. Hobbes not only considered the theory of war and the obligation of subjects to fight for the sovereign in his *Leviathan*, but he also wrote a contentious history of the English civil wars in *Behemoth*.[4] Thus, thinking about war in law, history, social philosophy, and the military arts themselves occupied the best minds of early modern society.

War and *society*, as the eighteenth-century encyclopedist Louis de Jaucourt realized, presented a paradox: "this state [of war] itself annihilates the state of society."[5] The *Encyclopédie* for which he wrote, billed as the work of a society of men of letters, was dedicated to Comte Marc-Pierre d'Argenson, the French secretary of state for war. Its grand design of explaining the principles and details of human knowledge included coverage of military arts and crafts as accomplishments of civilization. For Jaucourt, some wars were clearly justified in self-defense: "anyone who declares himself our enemy with a weapon in his hand, authorizes us to act against him with acts of hostility, damage, destruction, and death." And although there was some agreement on acts prohibited by "the military laws of Europe"—the killing of prisoners of war, old men, women and children, and "outrages to the honor of women"—there were still many shameful horrors suffered during wartime when the civil laws were silent. Some regulation of this destructive force was necessary. Earlier in the century perhaps the most idealistic proposal came from Abbé Charles-Irénée Castel de Saint-Pierre, a would-be

[4]"Hereby it is manifest that during the time men live without a common power to keep them all in awe, they are in that condition which is called war; and such a war, as is of every man, against every man." Thomas Hobbes, "Of the Natural Condition of Mankind as concerning their Felicity, and Misery," *Leviathan* (London: Andrew Crooke, 1651), pt. 1, chap. 13. *Behemoth, or an Epitome of the Civil Wars of England* was first published in 1679.

[5]D. J. [Louis, Chevalier de Jaucourt], "Guerre," *Encyclopédie, ou dictionnaire raisonné des arts, sciences, et métiers . . .*, ed. Denis Diderot (Paris: Chez Briasson, David l'Aîné, Le Breton, Durand, 1751–65), 7:985–98, quotation from 997. This volume was published in 1757 and refers to the contemporary war.

soldier whose weak health had required him to choose a clerical career. Saint-Pierre had attended the negotiations in 1712–13 for the Peace of Utrecht, and he put forward a project for a league of sovereigns, with a tribunal and a permanent congress to guarantee the peace. He attributed this idea to Henri IV of France (1553–1610), and thought that the good sense of his proposals would win general approval.[6] Whether any king ever seriously considered these notions is doubtful, but the reforming ideals of Saint-Pierre certainly have attracted a devoted following ever since they were first published. The longing for peace echoed in the writings of *philosophes* throughout the century: Montesquieu, Rousseau, Voltaire, and likewise Kant in *Toward Perpetual Peace* (1795) struggled to find answers to the social problem of war.[7]

Yet much as an eighteenth-century gentleman might sympathize with those who sought to regulate war or to abolish it entirely, he had only to read his gazettes to learn of the most recent engagements, and he was quite likely to know lawless soldiers and sailors even if he had not commanded them himself. Civil society, formed to prevent anarchic fighting among human beings, was constantly asking them to participate in organized fighting on its behalf. Professional soldiers serving the monarchs of Britain, France, Prussia, and Austria seemed less troubled by this situation, as did those intrepid conquerors of colonial peoples who were in the service of trading companies in Africa, America, and Asia. But the enlightened founders of new nations had their doubts: the moral test of

---

[6]Charles-Irénée Castel de Saint-Pierre, *Projet pour rendre la paix perpétuelle en Europe* . . . (Utrecht [Paris]: Antoine Schouten, 1713–17). Cardinal Dubois thought Saint-Pierre's ideas were "the dreams of a well-intentioned man," a title later adopted for an edition of his collected works: *Les rêves d'un homme de bien, qui peuvent être réalisés* . . . (Paris: Veuve Duchesne, 1775).

[7]Elizabeth V. Souleyman, *The Vision of World Peace in Seventeenth and Eighteenth Century France* (New York: Putnam, 1941). Werner Bahner, "Der Friedensgedanke in der Literatur der Französischer Aufklärung," in *Grundpositionen der Französischer Aufklärung*, ed. Werner Krauss and Hans Mayer (Berlin: Rutten and Loening, 1955), pp. 139–207, 301–17. Ira O. Wade, *The Structure and Form of the French Enlightenment*, 2 vols. (Princeton: Princeton University Press, 1977), 1:317–33.

Corsican, Irish, and American independence movements was how well their supporters would voluntarily arm themselves and rally to the cause. The use of experienced professional fighting men essential to victory was seen as corrupt in itself and corrupting to the movement's ideals.[8] How could political virtue be preserved without recourse to arms? By the last decade of the century, the French revolutionaries, those ardent supporters of citizen participation, came to believe that a society striving for justice and equality in a hostile world was particularly vulnerable to attack and would need organized armed forces both to defend itself and to spread the benefits of national liberation to its neighbors. It might also be necessary to inspire the citizens of the republic to greater sacrifices, "to force them to be free."[9] Thus war and society, in a striking resolution of the paradox, were inextricably linked in a philosophical and practical bond.

Were these wars profitable to those who started them? Surely the aggressors hoped to gain trading rights, cities, provinces, colonies, or even a crown—and sometimes they were successful. The objects of their desire, located in those unhappy frontier zones of northern Italy, Silesia, Bohemia, the Rhineland, and the southern Netherlands, paid the highest price for wars as they suffered armed invasion year after year. One wonders how their civilian populations survived such depredations, though there was some difference in damages caused by armies simply passing through and by those staying to occupy the land and do battle there. The truly catastrophic civilian losses occurred when war was joined with poor harvests and outbreaks of disease.[10] For the rulers, miscalculations

[8]Charles Royster, *A Revolutionary People at War: The Continental Army and American Character, 1775–1783* (Chapel Hill: University of North Carolina Press, 1979).

[9]Jean-Jacques Rousseau, *The Social Contract* (first ed., *Du contrat social*, Amsterdam: M. M. Rey, 1762), bk. 1, chap. 7. The practical import of these words can be seen in histories of the reign of terror, especially the works of Richard Cobb. The arguments of Jacob L. Talmon, who saw in Rousseau *The Origins of Totalitarian Democracy* (London: Secker and Warburg, 1952), are less persuasive.

[10]Myron Gutman, *War and Rural Life in the Early Modern Low Countries* (Princeton: Princeton University Press; Assen: Van Gorcum, 1980).

and reverses in battle certainly called the rationale of war into question. Political pamphleteers who thought little of the costs nonetheless urged nations to fight on, even when the original ends were lost in obscurity or had become most difficult to attain. Battle-weary Europe had enough of the War of Spanish Succession long before the treaties were signed in 1713–14. Louis XIV was seeking a negotiated peace as early as 1706 and even more strongly by 1709; a peace party had taken over the British government in 1710; and the Habsburg claimant to the Spanish throne, unable to conquer Spain, had inherited another empire in 1711. Yet even the irenic philosopher Gottfried Wilhelm Leibniz wrote vitriolic pamphlets demanding continuation of the war and condemning the "inexcusable" Peace of Utrecht.[11] At the other end of the century, Edmund Burke's intemperate *Letters on a Regicide Peace* (1796–97) showed the least appealing face of his conservatism. In his view, the economically devastating war against the French Revolution had to be continued because there could be no peace with king killers, atheists, divorcés, and cannibals.[12] As the bank robber who had not envisioned the desertion of his accomplices, the death of bystanders, or the timely arrival of the police, an eighteenth-century ruler who sought to grab territory might rue the consequences of his own temerity. In 1709, facing the humiliating demands of his enemies, Louis XIV no longer saw high aims in the struggle to preserve the Spanish inheritance of his grandson Philip V: "The principal object

[11]"La paix est fort bonne en soy, / J'en conviens, mais à quoy sert-elle / Avec des ennemis sans foy?" (Peace in itself is very good / I agree, but what is it worth / With faithless enemies?), in Gottfried Wilhelm Leibniz, "Réflexions d'un Hollandois sur la lettre contre les soupirs de l'Europe," p. 60; and see "Paix d'Utrecht inexcusable," composed 1712–14, excerpts and commentary in Petronella Fransen, *Leibniz und die Friedensschlüsse von Utrecht und Rastatt-Baden,* dissertation, Leiden, 1933 (Purmerend: J. Muusses, 1933).

[12]Burke charged the French revolutionaries with murder, divorce, irreligion, and cannibalism; he thought England was fighting for the cause of humanity and Christianity. "Perhaps it were better I had never written at all; but I had this to say or nothing." Burke to Mrs. John Crewe, November 23, 1796, *The Correspondence of Edmund Burke* (Cambridge: Cambridge University Press; Chicago: University of Chicago Press, 1970), 9:129.

of the present war is commerce of the Indies and the wealth they produce," he reportedly said, emphasizing the significance of empire.[13] Frederick the Great of Prussia, in the darkest days of the third Silesian war of 1757, wrote a regretful *Apology* to be published in the event of his death:

> How could I foresee that France would send 150,000 men into the Empire? How could I foresee that the Empire itself would declare war against me, that Sweden would also get involved in this war, that France would subsidize Russia, that England despite its guarantees would not support Hannover, furthermore that Holland would allow France and Austria to form an alliance, and that Denmark would see Russia and Sweden as equally guilty; in short, that the English would abandon me? . . . What pitiful people we are! The world judges our conduct not according to our intentions, but rather according to the consequences. What is left for us? A man must have good fortune.[14]

Of course Frederick lived to fight many another day, and his momentary regrets did not make him a pacifist.

Cost-benefit analysis of early modern wars is difficult because of incomplete and imprecise statistics. Money was often collected and spent without controls at every level of government. National budgets were rudimentary approximations at best, but the effects of wars are plainly visible, *grosso modo*. Although the national wealth increased in Britain from 1702 to 1713, the War of Spanish Succession required tripling both public expenditure and the national debt. The Seven Years' War (1756–63) cost the British government £160 million, of which some £60 million had to be borrowed.[15] The War of Austrian Succession (1740–48) forced the French government to resort to extraordinary fiscal expedients, including the

---

[13]Quoted by Ragnhild M. Hatton, *Europe in the Age of Louis XIV* (London: Thames and Hudson, 1969), p. 215, n. 8.

[14]Frederick II, King of Prussia, "Apologie de ma conduite politique," *Oeuvres de Frédéric le Grand* (Berlin: Rodolphe Decker, 1846–57), 27: 3, pp. 279–86. Ger. tr. "Rechtfertigung meines politischen Verhaltens," *Die Werken Friedrichs des Grosses* (Berlin: Reimar Hobbing, 1913), 3:213–15.

[15]Briggs, *Social History*, pp. 158, 167.

then-radical notion of income tax. And the War of American Independence (1776–83), a minor venture for the French in comparison to British efforts, set in motion a ruinous pattern of deficit spending, which formed an important part of the financial crisis of the monarchy, as Finance Minister Charles Alexandre de Calonne told Louis XVI in 1786.[16] Over the century as a whole, the British national debt rose from £14.2 million in 1700, to £130 million in 1763, and finally to £456 million in 1800. Indeed, debt service alone ran to £20 million per year by 1801—almost twenty times the entire annual expenditure of the Restoration state of Charles II.[17] This was an increase far in excess of the rate of inflation, and much of it should be attributed to warfare. But these costs of war were accepted as necessary:

> In great empires the people who live in the capital, and in provinces remote from the scene of action, feel, many of them scarce any inconveniency from the war; but enjoy, at their ease, the amusement of reading in the newspapers the exploits of their own fleets and armies. To them this amusement compensates the small difference between the taxes which they pay on account of the war, and those which they had been accustomed to pay in time of peace. They are commonly dissatisfied with the return of peace, which puts an end to their amusement, and to a thousand visionary hopes of conquest and national glory, from a longer continuance of the war.[18]

Adam Smith went on to say that the return of peace was seldom accompanied by a reduction in taxes or repayment of public debts in proportion to their wartime increase.

Not all military spending went up in smoke or down in drink, however, and contemporaries did not necessarily see it as wasteful.

[16]Marcel Marion, *Histoire financière de la France depuis 1715*, vol. 1 (Paris: A. Rousseau, 1914); Jean Egret, *La Pré-révolution française* (Paris: Presses Universitaires de France, 1962).

[17]Roy Porter, *English Society in the Eighteenth Century* (Harmondsworth: Penguin, 1982), p. 132.

[18]Adam Smith, "Of publick Debts," *An Inquiry into the Nature and Causes of the Wealth of Nations*, 2 vols., ed. R. H. Campbell, A. S. Skinner, and W. B. Todd (Oxford: Clarendon, 1976), bk. 5, chap. 3, 2:920.

It was an old dictum of political economy that trading nations should expect wars and even find them profitable so long as they were not fought on the home territory.[19] Indeed, according to Charles Wilson, " 'wars of limited liability,' . . . waged almost everywhere except on English soil," were understood as a natural corollary of expanding British trade.[20] Imports and exports flourished under the projection of imperial power. The best defense against French threats to this trade was a policy of maritime supremacy and attack, coupled with a diversion of the enemy to continental warfare. Even if this policy led to protracted war several times in the century, the costs were not regarded as too high in the age of industrial revolution. War itself had some economic advantages. Whether obtained by higher taxation or borrowing, money for war went back into circulation through government spending and stimulated technology, production, and employment. Military commissions, bureaucratic offices, lucrative contracts, high grain prices, and financial speculation might even generate a species of wartime prosperity at home, imperiled by threats of peace. Fear of the adverse economic consequences of peace was as common in 1713 as in 1815 or in 1919.

Thus the relationship of war and society in the eighteenth century was neither simply destructive nor constructive in its effects. Thinkers were forced to reflect on the strengths and weaknesses of an international order that repeatedly broke down. Some, like Adam

[19]Indeed, foreign war might even be prudent: "No man who loves his Countrey can grudge the Expence [of war abroad], because we are thereby preserved from the Devastations, Plunderings, Sackings, Burning and Slaughter, which we must have been Subject to, if the Seat of War had not been kept out of our own Countrey." A Merchant [Simon Clement], *A Discourse of the General Notions of Money, Trade, and Exchanges* . . . (London: n.p., 1695), p. 18. See also *The Present War No Burthen to England* (London: n.p., 1692), quoted in Orest A. Ranum and Patricia M. Ranum, eds., *The Century of Louis XIV* (New York: Harper and Row, 1973), pp. 299–304.

[20]Charles Wilson quotes Josiah Child (1630–99), "Profit and Power ought jointly to be considered," and relates this view to Pitt's system, in *England's Apprenticeship, 1603–1763* (London: Longman, 1965; 1979), pp. 281–87.

Ferguson, professed to see value in war as a force for social unity,[21] while others saw war, the antithesis of civilization, as a call for a new order. Financiers and economists knew the ruinous cumulative effects of military taxation and public debt, yet they were attracted by both short- and long-term advantages of war in spurring national production and assuring commercial dominance. Finally, monarchs and ministers had to balance their particular interests in acquiring territories and trade with those of their states in maintaining or breaking the peace of Europe.

Great considerations of the causes and course of wars still occupy historians and social scientists of our own day.[22] The ten essays in this volume contribute to this discussion by presenting evidence and arguments from specific cases. They represent a selection of papers read at the tenth Wilburt S. Brown Conference in History, held at The University of Alabama, February 11–12, 1983; and they have since been revised and edited for publication. The authors emphasize that eighteenth-century warfare, while limited by structural constraints of time and space mediated through technology, resulted from human choices, for better or for worse. Warfare, properly considered as an institution of society as well as its negation, required changes in peacetime ways of doing things. To fight wars successfully, armies and states had to adapt to conditions, whether in the American wilderness, the Caribbean, or the border regions of

[21]"The sense of a common danger, and the assaults of an enemy, have been frequently useful to nations, by uniting their members more firmly together, and by preventing the secessions and the actual separations in which their civil discord might otherwise terminate." Adam Ferguson, "Of the principles of war and dissension," *An Essay on the History of Civil Society*, 4th ed. (London: Caddel, 1773), pt. 1, sec. 4, p. 35.

[22]Quincy Wright, *A Study of War* (Chicago: University of Chicago Press, 1942). John U. Nef, *War and Human Progress: An Essay on the Rise of Industrial Civilization* (Cambridge: Harvard University Press, 1950). John Keegan, *The Face of Battle* (New York: Vintage/Random House, 1977). William H. McNeill, *Pursuit of Power: Technology, Armed Force, and Society since A.D. 1000* (Chicago: University of Chicago Press, 1982). Michael Howard, *The Causes of Wars* (Cambridge: Harvard University Press, 1983).

Europe itself. The strong historical current of interest in war and society in early America is reflected in the predominance of papers; for Europeans this other hemisphere was often the stage for local skirmishes in global conflicts.[23] Spanish, French, and British forces sent to America were of necessity more independent and less closely supervised from the capitals than troops in the Netherlands and the Pyrenees. Commanders received general orders from the mother country and were expected to carry them out with resources at hand. When the view from afar did not take adequate account of local conditions, as in the Cartagena expedition of 1740–42 or the attempt to capture Fort Duquesne in 1755, the results were disastrous. Several such disastrous expeditions might be necessary before commanders in the field realized and were able to persuade higher authorities that they had to adapt to conditions; several disastrous campaigns could throw the best diplomatic plans for war into complete disarray—and the outcome into doubt.

To perceptive contemporary observers, these truths might be self-evident, and yet there was considerable argument about how and where to project military power. European frontiers had to be defended through garrison towns like Perpignan, not only against the traditional enemy across the border, but also against civil insurrection by a recently acquired population of doubtful loyalty. Claude C. Sturgill shows that the costs of garrison defense were extremely high and that the economic effects of military presence in the town were great. The French army was by far the greatest consumer and employer, even in peacetime: it drew heavily on the hinterlands for food, supplies, fodder, animals, and men. Could a group of widely separated Caribbean garrisons provide similar security in the colonies and along trade routes? John R. McNeill notes the particular ecological and epidemiological conditions of the area, which gave well-established defending forces an advantage

---

[23]Douglas E. Leach, *Arms for Empire: A Military History of the British Colonies in North America, 1607–1763* (New York: Macmillan, 1973). John E. Ferling, *A Wilderness of Miseries: War and Warriors in Early America* (Greenwich, Conn.: Greenwood, 1980).

over attackers. If in Europe fortifications were designed to withstand siege until relief armies arrived to do battle with the attackers, in the Caribbean strong fortifications allowed the defenders to hold out until their attackers were decimated by disease, gave up, and withdrew. Douglas E. Leach provides a spirited account of one such affair, the Cartagena expedition. Everything that could have gone wrong in planning and execution certainly did, and despite the initial enthusiasm and bravery of the troops, the failure to adapt led to a sorry tale of misery, high casualties, and hard feelings between the British and their colonial allies.

The most comprehensive account of adaptation in the course of campaigns appears in Daniel J. Beattie's essay on the British army in North America during the Seven Years' War. Starting with another failed attempt to capture a frontier garrison, General Benjamin Braddock's march to Fort Duquesne in 1755, Beattie demonstrates that capable commanders eventually learned how to deal with wilderness conditions, in particular problems of supply and tactics. Success against the French and their Indian allies came only when the British developed more efficient transport services, chains of sturdy frontier forts, and companies of rangers and light infantry trained to fight and survive in the backwoods manner. Meanwhile, the prosperous inhabitants of more civilized coastal towns such as Newport, Rhode Island, also saw their trading activities affected by this war. As Sheila L. Skemp shows, they could not continue business as usual, and had to adapt by seeking naval protection for their ships, trading through neutral ports, privateering, or evading official restrictions entirely. Despite some individual success stories, the overall picture of wartime adaptation in Newport suggests that its trade, once interrupted, was irretrievably lost, and that its traders lost their own entrepreneurial spirit. Warfare thus played an important role in the economic decline of the town.

When the sounds of battle trumpets and cannons faded away into peace, other social problems of adaptation arose as reminders of war. Foremost among these was rewarding those who had served in the armed forces or in supporting civilian positions. Two of our essayists deal with this aspect of war and society in the eighteenth century. First, Robin F. A. Fabel examines the scheme for colonizing west Florida with New England veterans of the Seven Years' War. The would-be settlers regarded land grants as just compensation for their military service, none the less attractive despite the long delays in getting permission from London. Fabel explains the difficulties faced in the southern wilderness by emigrants from Connecticut and the attempts at adaptation that turned into a losing struggle for survival. This account of the Company of Military Adventurers reminds us also that the story of westward expansion in North America was not a series of uninterrupted triumphs over nature and the indigenous inhabitants. In another study of rewards for service, Douglas Clark Baxter looks at requests for pensions made by civilian employees of the French ministry of war. These clerks, often from families of dedicated officeholders, served the Crown for thirty, forty, fifty years and more. Before the emergence of a modern civil service with fixed rights to retirement and pensions, employees had to petition individually for recognition. Their reasons for claiming pensions included length of service, personal sacrifice, fidelity, and exactness in arduous tasks—all honorable claims in the courtly ancien régime. Baxter points out that the expansion of the service and precedents over the century led to informal guidelines and that the expectations of these men foreshadow the professionalism of civil service in the following century.

The last three essays in the volume deal with aspects of the American War of Independence, 1775–83. Lawrence E. Babits argues that General Nathanael Greene's strategy in the campaign of 1780–81 was based on his adaptation to the geography of the Carolinas. Following his experience as quartermaster general to the Continental army, Greene carefully considered the best means of supplying his own troops and of disrupting the supplies of his British opponents. Greene's firm control of transport by land and water ensured his success. At the beginning of the war, Richard L. Blanco suggests, the Continentals had given little thought to the medical needs of their army. When wounded men from the early battles overwhelmed the hastily improvised medical service, dramatic reorganization was necessary. The first attempts to provide adequate hospitals encountered both financial and political difficulties, but as the war continued measures were taken to improve the health and fighting effectiveness of all troops, with striking results. Finally, Charles Royster considers the interaction of war and American society over the long term. In the eighteenth century, war attended the creation of the American republic; then, and on several other occasions in American history, it shaped society to the present acceptance of standing armed forces with professional leadership and ultimate civilian control. In the last analysis, not only was warfare adapted to conditions in America, but also American society with its voluntaristic, participative ideals was adapted to the conditions of fighting wars.

The French Army in Roussillon, 1716–1720

CLAUDE C. STURGILL

It should go without saying that the royal army was as much part of French society in the eighteenth century as any other group within the kingdom. But, as this statement is not generally accepted by historians with antimilitary biases or simply not raised by those who believe that the old regime was corrupt from beginning to end, it must be explained again and again. The need for my colleagues to transcend their educated prejudices, formed at least in part by national revolutions or wars of independence, is the reason I have undertaken this study. It forms part of a more general audit of French military budgets from 1715 to 1789, which includes searching out even minor receipts, bills, and ledgers within various levels of administration. This research, now more than half complete, shows that in order to understand the French army during the eighteenth century historians must start from the premise that the army was a microcosm of old regime society, just as our twentieth-century armies represent the nations that field them.

It simply will not do to present the French army of this period as a band of drunken malcontents, running around Europe sounding trumpets, beating drums, and grabbing women. This army consisted of 140,000 effectives, of which 100,000 were French subjects and the rest mercenaries. We should think of 200 battalions, with

25,000 career officers added to the total of effectives, ultimately commanded by some 3,000 generals, exactly 12 of whom were marshals of France. For the administration, there were 167 commissioners of war plus their staffs in the war office and scattered throughout the kingdom. And there were many, many subgroups and functionaries, far more numerous than can be listed here. Altogether, between 1718 and 1720, this army represented approximately 25 percent of the annual expense of the government of France. Each year during peacetime the Crown bought, on average, 450,000 uniforms, 65,000 muskets, 11,000 horses, 300,000 pairs of boots, and 109,500,000 rations. These figures do not include units of the royal household, personal guards of important men and women of state, and special units, all of which were paid from a separate budget. We must accept the French army of the eighteenth century for what it was: the largest single industry in France.

All money expended from the budget of the secretary of state for war passed through the hands of the 167 commissioners, who were largely responsible for preparing the war budget each year.[1] They saw to proper disbursement of funds in each intendancy. Holding much the same authority within the military administration as the intendants did in the generalities, these men were spread around France in about thirty-five districts, each closely supervised by the war office in Paris and double-checked by the intendants. This essay is the first modern presentation of these administrators as an effective part of the daily operations of royal government.

Under normal circumstances, good office procedure requires that paper move from left to right within the same level of organization and up or down to higher or lower levels of responsibility, as required to solve various problems. However, within the accounting system of the French royal army during the eighteenth century, run by commissioners at various levels, the practice was somewhat different. When a commissioner of war inspected a troop unit,

---

[1]Claude C. Sturgill, *Le Financement de L'Armée de Louis XV, 1715–1730* (Paris: Service Historique de l'Armée de Terre, 1985).

fortress, or hospital, he exercised his dual function as inspector general and paymaster general. His monthly written reports of strength, morale, combat readiness, and equipment were copied and dispatched to the unit commander, the intendant of the generality, the war office, and the local garrison commander or general commanding in the field. On receipt of reports from all units at the central war office, the commissioners there prepared payment orders for pay and allowances and orders for all necessary supplies; these, after being copied several times, went to the office of the *commissaire extraordinaire des guerres* and from him back to the commissioners in the provinces for appropriate action.

All payments at the local level were carefully recorded in large folio account ledgers listing all money arriving from the central government and all disbursements down to the last penny. These *comptes* were kept by every commissioner who paid out funds. They are indeed exact accountings: it is difficult to find fault with their completeness or with the mathematical method of arriving at the *quitte*.

It is surprising in light of the vast surviving documentation that no one heretofore has tried to describe this system, even on the local level, let alone for the entire kingdom. This lacuna in French military scholarship may be explained partly by the scattering of materials among Parisian and provincial archives and private collections. However, the key to the materials is found in the Archives de la Guerre, in cartons labeled "Projects des Fonds, 1715–1789";[2] these are actual budgets of the *commissaire extraordinaire des guerres*, along with many working papers prepared every year by the war office. The materials not in Paris, save for a small section of the Archives Nationales, are actual *comptes* kept in each of the intendancies and the bills and receipts to prove the ledgers.[3]

[2]Archives de la Guerre, Y^a 57–67.
[3]These account ledgers are located in the Archives de la Guerre, series A1, A3, and 1K38; Archives Nationales, Z^{1}c; and series C of the Archives Départementales (hereafter cited as A.D.) of Aveyron, Côte-d'Or, Doubs, Hérault, Ille-et-Vilaine, Marne, Orne, Puy-de-Dôme, Pyrenées-Orientales, and Seine-et-Maritime.

Nowhere else in France does there exist so complete a file of the *comptes* as in the Archives Départementales des Pyrenées-Orientales in Perpignan.[4] The file is complete from 1715 to 1777 and nearly so until 1789. Here, in old Roussillon and the Comté de Foix, the modern historian can calculate the army's local economic impact with remarkable accuracy. In this essay it is not possible to present a quantitative analysis of all these expenditures even for a short period such as 1715–30; a complete study will have to await the labors of a French graduate student in Perpignan who is preparing his thesis for the state doctorate.

What can be accomplished here is an analysis of types of expenditures that the Crown made for pay and allowances of its garrisons in this area for the years 1716–20.[5] During this short period, the War of Spanish Succession had ended, and the size of the French army had been reduced from 400,000 to 140,000 by mid-1716. The Little War with Spain was fought from quartermaster-ordnance headquarters located in Perpignan, while the Plague of Marseille was yet to come. Thanks to the activities of John Law, the government had enough coin to pay its bills. Finally, the gradual buildup of military forces for the War of Polish Succession would not really begin until the summer training camps of 1727. Thus it can be argued that the period 1716–20 was a fully funded era, a very short period in which the military administration operated under "normal" conditions, possibly the only period of its kind for France in the eighteenth century.

Two remarkable figures showing the economic impact of the French army in Roussillon stand out prominently: first, the total amount paid out from 1716 to 1720 by the commissioner of war at Perpignan—9,470,813 *livres*; second, the portion spent in Roussillon and the Comté de Foix, approximately 90 percent of the total—8,516,478 *livres*. These are enormous sums, spent in a region of

---

[4]A.D., Pyrenées-Orientales, C 1–125, contain these account ledgers for the entire period 1715–89. The supporting bills and receipts are scattered throughout series C, but see especially C 126–215 and C 251–65.

[5]Ibid.

France that was *not* one of the more wealthy or populous.[6] Roussillon has high mountains and low population density. Like its coun-
terpart on the Atlantic side of the Pyrenees, the intendancy of
Roussillon was not considered rebellious, but the royal administration and garrisons were certainly watchful for any indication of a
renewed Catalan independence movement.

The military garrisons had always played an important role in the
history of Roussillon and the Comté de Foix. At least from Roman
times the military route from Barcelona to Marseille had come
through Roussillon, passing by the fortress complex at Perpignan.
Charlemagne had used this route and had staged his army at
Perpignan for his famous invasion of Spain. The only other viable
military land route lay through the eastern Pyrenees from Lérida in
Spain, past Bourg Madame and Mount Louis, down the Têt River,
which again ended facing the military garrison in Perpignan. The
only practicable invasion route from the Mediterranean was blocked
by the extensive fortifications at Collioure. Smaller, but well-kept,
defensive strong points at Villefranche, Prats de Mouillon, Fort de
Bains, St. Laurens de Cerda, and Fort de Verches certainly gave
Roussillon and the Comté de Foix the complexion of a single large
garrison town as well as providing places where an invader would
suffer large losses to move his troops through narrow mountain
passes, disembark in small harbors, cross a river, or cut the main
military route to Marseille. In any such well-garrisoned area the
local economy is greatly dependent on military expenditures for any
semblance of economic prosperity.

The massive sums reported above did not include such items as
fourrages, *étappes*, and other local charges. The totals were only for
*subsistance et entretement des troupes aux appointemens, suplément d'appoin-
temens, solde, et masse.*[7] And the totals were not raised through local
taxation, for the entire sum paid to the government headed by the

[6]"Les Mémoires des Intendants de 1696," Bibliothèque Nationale, Paris, MS.
français, 2205–2221.
[7]Title pages, A.D., Pyrenées-Orientales, C 43–51.

intendant did not exceed 1,703,296 *livres,* or less than 20 percent of the expenditures.[8]

Of course not all inhabitants of the intendancy would benefit from military spending in their region. However, it is certain that local economies within the buying range of company captains and soldiers were fatter and larger than they would have been without the garrisons. From the registers studied it is possible to locate nine areas that benefited to a large extent from military payrolls. These were Perpignan, Collioure, Mount Louis, Bellegarde, Villefranche, Prats de Mouillon, Fort de Bains, St. Laurens de Cerda, and Fort de Verches.[9]

Certainly the garrisoning of troops such as a battalion of infantry, a squadron of cavalry, or a battalion of artillery in a locale could mean the difference between great prosperity and near poverty for the population. Soldiers have always meant extra commerce and money. During this period, for example, each soldier was fed approximately 1,000 grams of bread, 500 grams of meat, 500 grams of legumes, 25 grams of cooking fats, and a liter of wine or beer per day. To feed his company, each infantry captain bought 35 times those amounts of each item. Just within the city of Perpignan, where 2,371 enlisted men were stationed in the infantry regiments of La Couronne and Rouergue and the artillery battalion of Raganne in 1718, the garrison officers bought the following amounts, *every day:* 2,371 kilos of bread, 1,185.50 kilos of meat and legumes, 59.28 kilos of cooking fats, and 2,371 liters of wine or beer.[10] The annual figures of consumption added to the local commerce of this city and its surrounding agricultural area are even more impressive (see Table 1). And one must not forget that the army of the old regime usually purchased daily rations for officers and uniforms, shoes, shirts, wood for cooking and heating, and so forth, at local markets. Furthermore, the salaries of retired officers, hospital staffs, *garde*

[8]"Histoire des finances pendant la Régence de 1715," Bibliothèque de l'Arsenal, Paris, MS. 4560.
[9]A.D., Pyrenées-Orientales, C 43–51.
[10]Ibid., C 46.

magasins, consignes des portes, garde artilleurs, and major Crown officers such as governors, lieutenants of the king, majors, assistant majors, and commanders for the king were added to the local economy and hence to the profits of the inhabitants.

Table 1: *Army Consumption at Perpignan, 1718*

Bread	865,415.00	kilograms
Meat	432,707.50	kilograms
Legumes	432,707.50	kilograms
Cooking Fats	21,635.38	kilograms
Wine/Beer	865,415.00	liters

The registers of the *commis de l'extraordinaire des guerres* show military expenditures in each area (see Table 2). These sums are just the money spent on foodstuffs and clothing by small-unit commanders such as infantry captains. Large sums also found their way into the local economy through local contractors operating under the bid system. These included:[11]

	1716	1717	1718	1719	1720
General Hospital	66,190	21,248	25,002	64,915	124,458
Wood and Candles	32,386	31,915	30,710	32,179	44,727
Bread		31,215	7,371	31,588	

The general hospital account appears to have included all medical expenses and salaries for one field and several fixed hospitals. The wood and candle account included lighting and heat for guard posts throughout the intendancy as well as wood for heating during winter. Normally, deductions from the daily pay of each soldier paid for the bread ration, but when the price of grain rose above normal levels, the king paid the difference.

[11]Ibid., C 43–51.

Table 2. *Military Expenditures in*
Roussillon and Comté de Foix[12]
(All sums have been rounded to the nearest *livre*.)

Region	1716	1717	1718	1719	1720
Perpignan	329,872	316,160	215,542	371,611	1,015,971
Collioure	154,756	154,653	159,670	177,306	232,900
Mount Louis	131,559	7,533	78,993	155,006	162,016
Bellegarde	70,504	86,664	96,919	140,252	161,379
Villefranche	30,749	37,995	17,101	60,063	60,687
Prats de Mouillon	34,072	29,735	18,574	44,411	52,388
Fort de Bains	7,291	9,785	6,622	12,315	15,415
St. Laurens de Cerda	1,500	1,500	1,500	1,500	1,500
Fort de Verches	1,400	1,400	1,400	1,400	1,400
Totals	761,703	645,425	596,321	963,864	1,703,656

There is yet a third category, best labeled pensions, from which money from the Crown was pumped into the local economy. Here, too, the payments were substantial:[13]

	1716	1717	1718	1719	1720
Retired officers attached to garrison	92,151	70,790	58,476	1,683	
Staff officers in various garrisons	42,276	37,880	39,110	38,743	44,068
Retired officers living in intendancy	9,481	9,485	7,022	6,430	3,608
Minor employees in various garrisons	2,228		10,017	23,714	23,768

[12]Ibid.
[13]Ibid.

These are only some of the categories of pensions paid within this area, but they represent all those paid to retired personnel who would spend their pensions locally.

Individual examples of money entering the economy of Roussillon and the Comté de Foix are very easy to come by. Below are several examples chosen from an almost unmanageable number of receipts and bills:[14]

- 2,630 *livres* for 70 new overcoats, 31 hand lanterns, and repairs to an additional 54 overcoats, to a tailor in Perpignan.

- 2,108 *livres* for 56,200 tent stakes and 1,054 *livres* for 14,050 bundles of brushwood, taken from a family's acreage near Mount Louis.

- 300 *livres* to several officers of the local militia, to return to their homes after their period of service.

- 947 *livres* for uniforms of a new battalion of *arquebusiers*.

- 480 *livres* per month for rental of two boats at Collioure for local coast guards.

- 200 *livres* per year to Catalan officials to give them means of living in France.

- 360 *livres* for 3 *quintaux* of gunpowder produced at Pamiers in the Comté de Foix.

- 2,709 *livres* for manufacture of beds.

- 70,000 *livres* for armament and uniforms of 2 full battalions of *arquebusiers*.

- 66 *livres* for rental of 2 mules for 10 days.

[14]Ibid., C 183.

And for some 10 percent of the total amount paid out by the *commis de l'extraordinaire des guerres* one cannot be sure that the money was spent in this generality. Among these questionable items are: (1) pay for winter quarters for officers who spent from three to five months in other parts of France; (2) pensions of officers of mountain troops: *miquelets, arquebusiers,* and *fusiliers de montagnes* (although these officers were usually residents of the intendancy, it is not possible to pinpoint their places of habitation); (3) appointments of chaplains, paid directly to local bishops; (4) appointments of general officers who were absent from their posts; (5) certain extraordinary expenses such as grants to permit officers to depart their stations for reasons of poor health, special pensions for services, money paid to members of the espionage network, money for prisoner exchanges, and reimbursements to the Maréchaussée and Prevotal courts for the capture, transportation, and costs of bringing deserters to justice.

Given this list of rather minor expenses, we may be justified in assuming that almost all of the 9,470,813 *livres* in the account ledgers was spent in the local economy; but until more detailed research confirms this, the 90 percent figure, 8,516,478 *livres,* may be proposed as the actual total of royal army expenditures in Roussillon and the Comté de Foix. During the period under discussion, 1716–1720, in an area where the civilian population could not have been more than 80–100,000 souls, the military garrison never fell below the 8–10,000 mark. In other words, for every ten civilians there was one soldier living in Roussillon and the Comté de Foix.[15] Can there be any doubt that the overall economic situation of the region would have been far worse without this military contribution?

[15]The population was estimated by the Royal Intendant in 1696. I have tried to provide for the natural increase and have taken into account such factors as the lack of widespread deaths from communicable diseases and foreign invasions to provide what I think is a reasonable population estimate. See "Les Mémoires des Intendants de 1696." For the numbers of the garrison, I have counted the men listed as present in the various ledgers of the *commissaires des guerres* but I have also allowed for men counted present who were unfit for duty for variable reasons: deserters, stragglers, and so forth. Experience with these account ledgers on a national scale has taught me to reduce such strength figures by approximately 5 percent from the official reports when clusters of three or more years are to be compared.

The Ecological Basis
of Warfare in the Caribbean,
1700–1804

JOHN R. McNEILL

*S*oldiers, sailors, physicians, and assorted civilians of past centuries knew that diseases regularly determined the outcome of battles and campaigns in tropical areas like the Caribbean, West Africa, and the East Indies. It is difficult for us, for whom most tropical diseases have become trivial, to imagine a world in which a soldier's most fearsome enemy was not his opponent but a variety of invisible infections. As accounts of almost any action show, however, this was clearly the case in the eighteenth-century Caribbean. Historians have not entirely ignored this characteristic of Caribbean warfare, but by and large they have not explained how it worked. Most have tended to assume that tropical disease operated arbitrarily and impartially.[1] They have followed their sources too closely, accepting pestilence as an act of God or nature, declining to consider

I should like to thank all those who have read and commented on this paper: John Cell, Barry Gaspar, Ann McDougall, William McNeill, Tom Magnuson, Theodore Ropp, Julius Scott, John TePaske, and Peter Wood.

[1]Cyril Hamshere, *The British in the Caribbean* (Cambridge: Harvard University Press, 1972), p. 186. Francisco Guerra, "The Influence of Disease on Race, Logistics, and Colonization in the Antilles," *Journal of Tropical Medicine and Hygiene* 69 (1966): 23–35. Guerra allows that disease showed partiality between races on the basis of acquired immunities.

that important patterns might emerge from an examination of the disease history of the Caribbean.

While both God and nature work in mysterious ways, these ways are not necessarily random. The workings of Caribbean disease in the eighteenth century were demonstrably nonrandom; indeed, they played a crucial role in preserving the international status quo in the Antilles throughout the century, and then an equally crucial role in disrupting the status quo in the Haitian revolution (1803–04). Without continual and reliable assistance from tropical disease, Spain would have lost its Caribbean holdings to Britain, and with them the ability to safeguard the precious metals of Mexico and Peru. The Spanish won their New World empire in the sixteenth century with decisive help from Eurasian diseases; they kept it in the eighteenth with the help of African ones.

The Disease Environment of the Caribbean. The roster of tropical diseases is a long one, but in the Caribbean the most important have been malaria and yellow fever. Both are communicated to human beings by mosquitoes, both produce dangerous fevers in their victims, but yellow fever is more lethal. "Yellow jack" to the English, *vómito negro* to the Spanish, *mal de Siam* or *fièvre jaune* to the French, yellow fever is a viral infection, probably native to the West African forest, where it troubles tree-dwelling monkeys more than humankind.[2] In its classic form, the disease cannot be transmitted from person to person but only through its vector, *Aedes aegypti*, a mosquito that carries the virus from one host to another.[3]

[2]See George K. Strode, ed., *Yellow Fever* (New York: McGraw-Hill, 1951), esp. pp. 233–98, 438–533. Henry R. Carter, *Yellow Fever: An Epidemiological and Historical Study of its Place of Origin* (Baltimore: Williams and Wilkins, 1931).

[3]Two caveats are in order here. First, what is called "jungle yellow fever" can be communicated to man from monkeys by other arthropods than the *A. aegypti*. This link has been the source of many outbreaks in South America. Second, casting man as host and mosquito as vector is an example of unscientific anthropocentrism. Human beings are quite transitory in the cycle of the virus: it spends most of its time in the salivary glands of mosquitoes and does most of its multiplication there as well. In truth, man is the vector that carries the virus from mosquito to mosquito. But I will follow traditional nomenclature here for the sake of clarity.

Because *A. aegypti* is a domesticated mosquito that breeds in water containers with artificial sides, such as casks or cisterns, it is found only where it can keep human company. Rarely traveling more than 300 meters from its birthplace, except aboard ship, the yellow fever mosquito does not enjoy swamps and puddles frequented by malarial mosquitoes (*Anopheles*). Yellow fever is thus predominantly an urban disease, generally confined to port cities, while malaria is preeminently a rural one, common almost wherever stagnant water and warm weather coincide. The range of yellow fever is limited by *A. aegypti*'s sensitivity to cold: the mosquito needs 80° Fahrenheit to prosper, 62° to feed, and 50° to avoid coma. Thus yellow fever could survive indefinitely only in the tropics, although in the eighteenth century it made seasonal forays as far north as Boston.

The yellow fever virus itself has certain requirements for survival, which further limit the potential range of the disease. First, the virus must establish a cycle that allows indefinite transfer from mosquito to human host to mosquito. Without a critical mass of *A. aegypti*, the virus will die out once the population of infected mosquitoes is exhausted. In the first case the virus will last only a few days, because human beings either die or develop antibodies very quickly; in the second case the virus will survive only a few weeks, because mosquitoes have short life spans averaging fifty days. The establishment of an indefinite cycle therefore requires both susceptible hosts and suitable vectors in sufficient quantity.

As far as human hosts are concerned, mere quantity is not enough. The cycle requires a sufficient ration of nonimmunes to immunes among the population on which infected mosquitoes feed, for if a mosquito feasts only on immune blood the cycle is broken upon the death of the infected mosquito. Thus the perpetuation of yellow fever in a community that is largely immune requires an extraordinary concentration of infected *A. aegypti*, but among a population with few immunes a much smaller number of infected mosquitoes will assure the survival of the virus. The intensity of an outbreak of yellow fever similarly is governed by these two factors: the absolute population of *A. aegypti* and the proportion of nonimmune human blood in an area where mosquitoes already carried the infection or, alternatively, the importation of the virus into a community where the proportion of nonimmune human blood was already sufficiently high.

The virulence of yellow fever distinguishes it from other Caribbean infections. An outbreak can bring 85 percent mortality among those infected. Although often mild in children, in susceptible adults yellow fever produces several grisly symptoms after an incubation of three to five days, and then either death or lifelong immunity after another three to seven days.

Malaria, the other great killer in the Caribbean, showed a much more thorough adaptation to human hosts. It killed far fewer of its victims and produced only temporary immunities in survivors. Thus it did not depend for its perpetuation on a fragile cycle, as did yellow fever, and consequently malaria was more common wherever conditions allowed species of *Anopheles* to flourish. Although a bout of malaria was less serious than one with yellow fever, malaria probably killed more people in the Caribbean because it could recur repeatedly.[4] Certain genetic traits, such as sickle cell, influence vulnerability to malaria, resulting in individuals bearing partial immunities even though they have never encountered the disease. But with yellow fever there is no easily conferred immunity, just as there is no cure.[5] One must survive the disease (or vaccination in the modern world) to be safe from it.

Most tropical diseases are tropical for reasons of temperature: either the pathogens or their carriers can survive only in comparatively warm environments. Their potential range is confined to permanently warm areas, like the lowland tropics, and places that

[4]Philip Curtin, "Epidemiology and the Slave Trade," *Political Science Quarterly* 83 (1968): 190–216, estimates that among British soldiers malaria killed three for every two deaths from yellow fever.

[5]Some historians examining differential death rates from yellow fever in the nineteenth-century American south conclude that blacks must somehow carry innate partial immunities to yellow fever. Medical science has no explanations. Kenneth Kiple and Virginia King, *Another Dimension of the Black Diaspora: Diet, Disease and Racism* (New York: Cambridge University Press, 1981), pp. 40–48.

are both seasonally hot and in close enough contact with the tropics
to permit transfer of infection. The Caribbean, West and Central
Africa, South Asia, and the East Indies have historically been loci of
tropical diseases. Regions such as southern Europe, coastal China,
and the eastern seaboard of North America suffered from tropical
infections only in the summer months and only in those summers
when the movement of ships and sailors brought diseases into
contact with susceptible populations.

In the annals of European warfare tropical infection was never so
decisive as in the eighteenth-century Caribbean. Why this particular
place and time? Prior to the twentieth century, the human traffic
connecting the Caribbean to the wider world created a corresponding microbiotic traffic much larger than in other tropical zones. In
the eighteenth century, the tremendous growth of colonial trade,
including the slave trade, intensified the interchange of diseases
between America, Europe, and Africa; and the Caribbean served as
the crossroads of contagion. Whereas during the seventeenth century vulnerable West Indian populations might be spared contact
with lethal pathogens, by the eighteenth century the more thorough
confluence of disease pools assured regular exposure to all major
infections. This escalation of what might be termed the velocity of
infection—analogous to the economists' velocity of money—did not
obtain to an equal degree in other tropical areas. West Africa, for
example, remained comparatively isolated despite the growing slave
trade.[6] While diseases in West Africa might have been more lethal to
those lacking appropriate immunities (and among Europeans the
death rates in West Africa in fact exceeded those in the Caribbean),[7]
the smaller number of susceptible hosts circulating within West
Africa, and the smaller number of ships bearing infected crews or
mosquitoes meant that West Africa was a less important domicile of
tropical infection than the Caribbean.

[6]Ibid., pp. 4–5.
[7]Curtin, "Epidemiology," p. 203.

The lethality of the Caribbean increased markedly from the seventeenth to the eighteenth centuries. The yellow fever virus probably first appeared in the West Indies not long before 1649, when an outbreak reduced the population of Havana by perhaps one-eighth.[8] But outbreaks remained sporadic thereafter until the 1690s, partly because human and microbiotic traffic remained slight by later standards. Brazil suffered from the disease in the 1680s, but yellow fever became commonplace in the West Indies only after a severe epidemic in the 1690s that was instigated by the arrival of a French ship at Martinique. The ship had come from Bangkok, thus the French misnomer *mal de Siam* although yellow fever is actually unknown in the Far East.[9] Actually it seems that the ship had taken aboard the virus on a stop in Recife, Brazil. After the 1690s, epidemics of yellow fever became routine in the Caribbean. The virus was often present and constantly reintroduced by ships' crews; *A. aegypti* flourished wherever people stored water in artificial containers. All that was needed to trigger epidemics was the influx of a large number of nonimmune hosts.

In the seventeenth century such influxes were rare. Population in the West Indies was so small and fortifications so undeveloped that conquests were often the work of a handful of buccaneers. Large expeditionary forces were unnecessary. The long absence of yellow fever, which allowed the birth and maturation of many nonimmunes, could build up the critical proportion to the point where a few infected mosquitoes could start an epidemic; the gradual immigration of European civilians could have the same effect. Indeed, on the southern shores of the Caribbean yellow fever often went by the name of *chapetonada* because it attacked *chapetones*, new immigrants. But before the 1690s, the introduction of the virus into vulnerable communities was rare. Not until the rapid expansion of shipping

---

[8]J. Le Roy y Cassa, *La primera epidemia de fiebre amarilla en la Habana* (Havana: "La Propagandista," 1930). Carter, *Yellow Fever*, pp. 187–92.

[9]Carter, *Yellow Fever*, p. 196. No convincing explanation exists for the absence of yellow fever in the Far East. *Aedes aegypti* existed, but not the virus. Strode, *Yellow Fever*, p. 532.

after 1713 did the velocity of infection increase to imperil every susceptible community.

Prior to the 1690s, yellow fever affected civilians as much as it did military personnel. But once the velocity of infection accelerated and the age of expeditionary warfare dawned, yellow fever emerged as a preeminently military matter, the arbiter of organized violence in the Caribbean. It continued in that role until the age of expeditionary warfare came to a close in the West Indies about 1825, when Spain lost its struggles with the new South American republics. Thereafter, yellow fever quietly resumed its career as a civilian menace. Death rates among soldiers declined, perhaps because European armies used proportionately fewer unseasoned troops, or perhaps because the yellow fever virus evolved a better adaptation to its host. Incidentally, the eventual solution to endemic yellow fever came as a result of the resumption of imperial conflict and expeditionary warfare in the Caribbean in the 1890s. The suffering of American troops during the Spanish-American War prompted efforts that led to Walter Reed's breakthrough. But after 1825, competition for dominion in the American tropics abated. When it resumed at the close of the century, the value to Europeans of the sugar islands had sufficiently declined so that the impact of yellow fever on warfare in the West Indies scarcely mattered. Henceforth it was primarily in Africa that tropical infection influenced the balance of power, this time not among European empires but between Africans and Europeans.

The Political and Military Environment of the Caribbean. How then did the violent and pitiless competition of microorganisms affect the violent and pitiless rivalry of European empires in the eighteenth-century Caribbean? The eighteenth century must be reckoned the climax of imperial expansion in the New World. Two centuries of competition for the fruits of empire left each state of Atlantic Europe with greater or lesser chunks of the Americas. Britain, France, and Spain uneasily divided the large and valuable Caribbean islands, always with an eye toward acquiring their rivals' possessions. The value of the French and British islands lay in their capacity to produce sugar for export to Europe; in the Spanish Caribbean sugar exports in the eighteenth century mattered less than the military value of the islands, although other agricultural activity, such as tobacco growing in Cuba, endeared the Caribbean colonies to the Spanish government. To the French and British, Caribbean colonies were the principal jewels in the crown of empire; to the Spanish, Caribbean colonies in general and Cuba in particular protected the mines of Mexico and Peru and the danger points along the seaways by which American treasure sailed to Spain.

By virtue of their economic and strategic value, the West Indies inevitably became a theater of battle when a European war broke out, and war broke out quite often in the eighteenth century because it was a perfectly acceptable arbiter of international disputes. The five major West European wars of the century all featured significant Caribbean dimensions, both at sea and ashore. In all, close to forty years of the century witnessed sustained campaigning. As war became commonplace, West Indian colonies required stout defenses. Fortified ports generally formed the basis of every island's defenses, because invaders invariably came by sea.

Long distances from Europe and demographic conditions in the West Indies created a pattern of warfare quite different from that which prevailed in Europe or indeed from that of the buccaneering days of the seventeenth century.[10] The comparative scarcity of whites and their implacable fear of arming blacks led to warfare by expeditionary force. Any attempted conquest in the Caribbean required massive accumulation and transportation of European men and supplies, careful coordination between armies and navies, and at least temporary command of the sea. For a whole host of reasons, France, Spain, and Holland effectively conceded naval superiority to Great Britain by 1713, so that Britain fielded far more expeditions

---

[10]For European war, see Michael Howard, *War in European History* (Oxford: Oxford University Press, 1976), chap. 4.

than the other powers.[11] Brief exceptions, notably during the War of American Independence, allowed the Bourbons to mount occasional expeditions of their own, but for the most part they found themselves in defensive roles, fighting to retain colonial possessions around the world from British predation. Sea power made the difference between the offensive and the defensive in far-flung theaters of war and often between victory and defeat as well—but not in the Caribbean.

Here the mere ability to transport large armies and their supplies could not guarantee success. The proper season for expeditions to the Caribbean began in winter, after the end of the hurricanes. The onset of the rainy season in May and June brought an increase in the populations of anopheles mosquitoes and consequently greater risk from malaria. So Europeans tried to conduct their attacks in the Caribbean in a five- or six-month period between December and May, thereby reducing the variety of dangers they faced. In any season, however, they risked an encounter with yellow fever, and by avoiding the rains they may actually have increased the risk, because *A. aegypti* probably increased during the dry months when people stored more water. Whatever the season, lethal infections so expanded the "killing zone"[12] that the normal considerations of land warfare in Europe did not apply: God was not on the side with the bigger battalions but rather on the side with the more disease-experienced troops. Soldiers died in camp, in their tents, and in field hospitals much more often than in actual fighting. Probably fewer than 10 percent of military deaths in the eighteenth-century Carib-

---

[11]See José P. Merino Navarro, *La armada española en el siglo XVIII* (Madrid: Fundación Universitaria Española, 1981); Georges Lacour-Gayet, *La marine militaire française sous le règne de Louis XV et sous la régence* (Paris: H. Champion, 1902); Michael Duffy, "The Foundations of British Naval Power," in Michael Duffy, ed., *The Military Revolution and the State, 1500–1800* (Exeter: University of Exeter, 1980), pp. 49–85.

[12]For an explanation of this concept, see John Keegan, *The Face of Battle* (London: Jonathan Cape, 1976).

bean are attributable to combat.[13] A brief look at mortality in Caribbean campaigns will demonstrate the appalling risks taken by European troops in the West Indies.

Caribbean Campaigns in the Eighteenth Century. European soldiers assigned to the West Indies could not expect to come home. Although their chances were better if they were sent out for garrison duty, that too was dangerous: in the eighteenth century, British garrison mortality in the West Indies averaged 20 percent annually.[14] Those who survived a year's service stood a three times greater chance of survival than newcomers. But the murderous effects of malaria and yellow fever showed most strikingly among the expeditionary forces. At Spanish Cartagena (in present-day Colombia) in the spring of 1741, about 77 percent of the besieging British troops died (70 percent if one includes the American colonials), very few of them in combat.[15] The valor of the Spanish defenders went almost untested. As John Fortescue, the historian of the British army, wrote, "Hostilities were simply extinguished by yellow fever."[16] Simply by holding out for several weeks the Spanish managed to destroy a British force of 10,000 men.

In 1780 another British expedition to the Spanish Main to a stronghold in present-day Nicaragua also lost 77 percent of its men,

[13]David Geggus, *Slavery, War and Revolution: The British Occupation of St.-Domingue, 1793–1798* (Oxford: Oxford University Press, 1982), p. 365, offers this figure for British troops in St.-Domingue, 1793–98.

[14]William Lemprière, *Practical Observations on the Diseases of the Army in Jamaica as They Occurred Between the Years 1792 and 1797*, 2 vols. (London: Longman and Rees, 1799), 1:160–232. Guerra, "Influence of Disease," p. 29; Hamshere, *British in the Caribbean*, p. 186.

[15]G. A. Kempthorne, "The Expedition to Cartagena," *Journal of the Royal Army Medical Corps* 44 (1936):270–77. Geggus, *Slavery, War and Revolution*, p. 364. Sir John Fortescue, *A History of the British Army*, 13 vols. (London: Macmillan, 1899–1931), 2:66–79. John J. Keevil, Christopher Lloyd, and Jack L. S. Coulter, *Medicine and the Navy, 1200–1900*, 3 vols. (Edinburgh and London: E. and S. Livingstone, 1957–63), 3:105. The most poignant description of the horror is in Tobias Smollett's *Roderick Random*.

[16]Sir John Fortescue, *The Empire and the Army* (London: Cassell, 1928), p. 73.

almost all to disease. Yellow fever forced the abandonment of an initially successful conquest. Among the few survivors was Horatio Nelson, the hero of Trafalgar a quarter of a century later.[17]

The British conquest of Havana in the summer of 1762 cost the victors 40 percent of their 14,000 troops, probably to a combination of yellow fever and malaria. In this siege the Spanish surrendered just as disease began to ravage the British forces; had the defenders held out another week or two, this British success would probably have become yet another failure. A year later, at the Peace of Paris, the British readily returned Havana to the Spanish, in large measure because experience had proved it a deadly place.[18]

Several other campaigns illustrate the decisive power of yellow fever and other pathogens in Caribbean conflicts: fever repulsed the British at Martinique in 1693, killing 75 percent of 2,400 men; the British lost 70 percent of 7,000 men in capturing, occupying, and abandoning three tiny French islands a century later; and the champion graveyard for European soldiers in the Antilles was St.-Domingue, the western third of the island of Hispaniola (Haiti after 1804).[19] Responding to the invitation of French planters, the

[17]Fortescue, *History of the British Army*, 3:344–46.

[18]Most historians credit yellow fever alone with this loss, but Geggus, *Slavery, War and Revolution*, p. 351, without evidence or explanation, ascribes it to malaria. Since the British camped out in marshy lowlands outside the urban area, malaria is a strong candidate, but there is good evidence for the introduction of yellow fever as well, inasmuch as some Spaniards within the city died of the fever also. See Carter, *Yellow Fever*, p. 192; Sir Noel Cantlie, *The History of the Army Medical Department*, 2 vols. (Edinburgh and London: Churchill Livingstone, 1974), 2:117–18. For the siege, Archivo General de Indias, Seville (hereafter cited as AGI), Seccion de Ultramar, legajo 169, contains forty-four letters from the governor, Juan de Prado; his siege journal is printed in Jacobo de la Pezuela y Lobo, *Diccionario geográfico, estadístico, histórico de la Isla de Cuba*, 4 vols. (Madrid: Mellado, 1863–66), 3:27–51. A fine account is in the introduction to David Syrett, ed., *The Siege and Capture of Havana, 1762* (London: Publications of the Navy Records Society, by Spottiswoode, Ballantyne, 1970).

[19]Since most expeditions were British, the best single source for narratives of these campaigns is Fortescue, *History of the British Army*, vols. 2–4. Guerra, "Influence of Disease," has brief accounts of many of these campaigns. A list of West Indian epidemics after 1650 appears in August Hirsch, *Handbook of Geographical and Historical Pathology*, 3 vols. (London: New Sydenham Society, 1883–86), 1:318–31.

British took and occupied most of St.-Domingue in 1793. In the next five years, 62 percent of the British troops sent there died, about 12,500 men in all, before the British finally abandoned the occupation. Four years later, in 1802, the French tried to reclaim the rebellious black colony for their empire. Napoleon's brother-in-law and 40,000 other Frenchmen died in this endeavor, as the Haitians intentionally avoided a decisive encounter and waited for yellow fever to destroy the invaders. Virtually none of the original French force of 25,000 survived.[20]

European fleets also suffered tremendous losses from yellow fever. The affinity of *Aedes aegypti* for water casks meant that many sea voyages carried the virus for as long as nonimmune blood lasted or until the ship sailed to colder climes. Yellow fever destroyed Rear Admiral Hosier's fleet in 1726–27, for example; and Admiral López Pintado's squadron suffered the same fate in 1730 before making it back to Cadiz and inaugurating the first yellow fever epidemic in Europe.[21]

In these instances, as in others at Portobello, Santiago de Cuba, and elsewhere, success or failure hinged on the speed with which tropical infection destroyed the nonimmune invading troops and sailors. If defenders could last long enough—generally six weeks sufficed—yellow fever virtually assured their triumph. Attackers had to reduce the enemy quickly or face almost certain defeat. Warfare in the Caribbean essentially boiled down to a race between the besiegers and the establishment of the man–mosquito yellow fever cycle. Servants of the British Crown in the West Indies understood the imperatives of this race. Admiral Charles Knowles wrote: "Whatever is to be effected in the West Indies must be done as expeditiously as possible, or the climate soon wages a more destructive War, than the Enemy."[22] A British military surgeon in 1780 explained the influence of disease on the conduct of warfare in

---

[20]Nicolas Pierre Gilbert, *Histoire médicale de l'Armée française à St.-Domingue* (Paris: Gabon, 1803).

[21]Keevil, Lloyd, and Coulter, *Medicine and the Navy*, 3:97–99.

[22]British Library, Additional Manuscripts, 23,678, fol. 17.

the Caribbean: "But delay should never be made in an attack for the reason that makes the Fabian maxim *cunctando* a certain defence in hot climates. . . . If the besiegers can be kept from possessing any town, or extensive buildings, they may be left to climate and the 'Tented field': for sickness will prevent European troops from succeeding in any attempt, where the service exceeds six weeks."[23]

Why did defenders not suffer equally from the ravages of yellow fever? In almost every port in the Spanish and French Caribbean yellow fever had become virtually endemic after the 1690s; mosquitoes were always present and maritime traffic constantly reintroduced the virus. What was missing for the establishment of the cycle was a sufficient proportion of nonimmunes. Precisely because of the continual presence of yellow fever, most colonists in the Caribbean, like West Africans, had been exposed to the disease when young and survivors carried lifelong immunity. The cycle could establish itself only among new immigrant communities, such as arriving armies, but not among the local population. Occasional outbreaks of yellow fever in West Indian ports normally signalled a momentary increase in the proportion of nonimmunes, but aside from expeditionary forces and occupying armies, this proportion rarely grew large enough to support epidemics.[24] Thus the incidence of yellow fever was anything but neutral in the eighteenth-century Caribbean. It systematically aided locals against outsiders; and given the international situation of the day and the prevailing mode of warfare, this meant the virus worked for the Spanish and French but against the British.

Implications of Disease for Caribbean Warfare. Many important implications derive from the partiality of yellow fever. For example, militia forces, by virtue of their Creole composition, contained comparatively few nonimmunes and thus enjoyed exemption from the usual

[23]Anonymous, *On Military Operations in the West Indies* (London: n.p., ca. 1782).
[24]The British colonization of Jamaica, 1655–70, and the French effort to settle Guyana, 1763–64, are examples of civilian migrations. Guerra, "Influence of Disease," pp. 32–33.

risk associated with large agglomerations of soldiers in the West Indies. This immunity encouraged their use not only in defensive capacities, the traditional militia role and all that militiamen bargained for, but for offensive operations as well. Their limited numbers, impatience with drill and discipline, and inadequate armament often made militia unsuccessful in combat with professional soldiery, but their resistance to disease compensated for their shortcomings. As tropical infections were much more lethal than combat, the ability to withstand disease often proved more important than martial prowess. Thus the Spanish chose to use Cuban militia in 1742 against Georgia—a region well within the malarial and yellow fever zones most months of the year—and they escaped serious harm from disease.[25] The white Creole population of Cuba—120,000 or so by 1762—made possible an extensive militia, leaving Spain to support a regular garrison only about one-third to one-tenth the size of the militia.[26] The racial composition of the French and British islands did not encourage extensive use of militia. Whites were few, and their proportion to blacks fell constantly throughout the century. Any suggestion that the home government should arm blacks met firm resistance from white Creoles. The Spanish did arm blacks in the eighteenth century but on a small scale; the balance of armed force always rested securely with whites in Cuba and Puerto Rico.[27] The French and British had occasionally used free blacks and slaves as military auxiliaries in the seventeenth century, and even raised black militia companies at times in the eighteenth, but not until the disastrous experiences of 1793–98 did either power experiment with

---

[25]Larry Ivers, *British Drums on the Southern Frontier* (Chapel Hill: University of North Carolina Press, 1974); Antonio de Bethencourt Massieu, "Felipe V y la Flórida," *Anuario de Estudios Americanos* 7 (1950): 95–123.

[26]AGI Santo Domingo 2104–05, 1201, 2107–08, 2093, and 2110–12 contain the *relaciones* on which this calculation is based.

[27]Pedro Deschamps Chapeaux, *Los batallones de pardos y morenos libre* (Havana: Editorial Arte y Literatura, 1976). Whites remained in the majority, enhancing their sense of security. See G. Douglas Inglis, "The Historical Demography of Cuba, 1492–1780" (Ph.D. diss., Texas Christian University, 1979).

slave soldiers in the West Indies. The decimation of British occupying forces in St.-Domingue and the French Lesser Antilles,
especially Martinique, Guadeloupe, and St. Lucia, directly precipi-
tated the "Africanization" of the British army beginning in 1795.[28]

Militia forces, and eventually slave soldiers, formed an important
segment in most Caribbean systems of defense. The Cuban militia
enjoyed the reputation of good fighters, an accolade rare for such
units. Its ability to fight when regular units lay prostrated by fever
accounted for its acclaim. In a set-piece conflict, of course, regular
troops would normally assert their superiority over militia in the
Caribbean as elsewhere, but in a protracted siege or campaign in the
hostile disease environment of the West Indies, the value of militia
vis-à-vis regular units was immeasurably greater.

The presence of yellow fever had other implications for the
conduct of warfare in the Caribbean. Protracted campaigns and
sieges became the rule because the vulnerability of expeditionary
forces to infection clearly increased the value of fortification. Samuel
Johnson was only half right when he wrote: "[The Spanish domin-
ions] are defended not by walls mounted with cannon which by
cannon may be battered, but by the storms of the deep and the
vapours of the land, by the flames of calenture and blasts of
pestilence."[29]

Actually, both pestilence and fortifications defended the Spanish
empire. Whereas a large and expensive Vauban-style fortress at a
place like Louisbourg, on Cape Breton Island in Nova Scotia, was
absurdly out of place and entirely at the mercy of attackers who
enjoyed command of the sea, stout fortifications in the West Indies
greatly improved the chances of successful defense. Eighteenth-cen-

[28]Roger N. Buckley, *Slaves in Red Coats: The British West India Regiments, 1795–1815*
(New Haven: Yale University Press, 1979), pp. ix, 1–19. Buckley says that Islamic
slave soldiers probably served as a model, but Indian sepoys must have been a more
familiar tradition to the British, and the French West Indian example after 1792 more
immediate.

[29]Samuel Johnson, "Thoughts on the Late Transactions Respecting Falkland's
Islands," in *Political Writings*, vol. 10 of *The Yale Edition of the Works of Samuel Johnson*,
ed. D. Greene (New Haven: Yale University Press, 1977), pp. 373–74.

tury European fortresses were not designed to be impregnable but rather to resist attackers for about six weeks, by which time (the theory went) relief columns could come to the rescue. In the Americas no such help would come within six weeks; indeed, for those without sufficient sea power, it might never come. But in the tropics the logic of fortification was upheld by *Aedes aegypti* and *Anopheles*, which regularly destroyed attackers much more thoroughly than Bourbon fleets and armies could have done. Sometimes the destruction came after the defenders had already given in, as at Havana in 1762, but the annihilation of occupying troops often forced evacuation of captured ports and islands, as at St.-Domingue in 1798.

Tropical disease so raised the value of fortification for Caribbean defense that the French and Spanish preferred to invest in masonry rather than ships. Ships had the great advantage of flexibility and mobility—they could serve offensively and defensively, in far-off imperial conflicts or in home waters. But they could not defend Caribbean possessions (or those anywhere in the tropics) as reliably as fortification could.

With yellow fever and malaria making Caribbean defense more reliable and less expensive, the French and Spanish could safely scrimp on their navies. This is not to argue that the decadence of the French navy after the 1690s is a direct result of the impact of disease considerations on imperial defense, for that would be stretching the evidence well beyond acceptable limits. Rather it is merely to point out that tropical disease reduced the strategic cost of saving on the navy and thus allowed the French and Spanish to devote more resources to continental ambitions, as both powers did in the eighteenth century. They certainly had other reasons not to compete with Britain in a naval arms race. Yellow fever probably never entered into the budget decisions made in Paris and Madrid, but it certainly improved the wisdom of the decisions taken.

Conclusion. The presence of tropical infections, and yellow fever in particular, dominated military events in the eighteenth-century

Caribbean, influencing strategy and tactics as well as results. Yellow fever radically changed the cost-effectiveness of militia versus regular troops and of fortifications versus ships. Given the shortage of loyal subjects in the slave societies of the West Indies, Europeans practiced war by expeditionary force, invariably bringing large concentrations of nonimmune blood within reach of the yellow fever vector, *Aedes aegypti.* The usual results were the deaths of thousands of European soldiers and insignificant or temporary change in the distribution of imperial holdings in the region. When locals began fighting to upset the status quo rather than to preserve it, as in the Haitian revolution, yellow fever no longer served to stabilize political relations in the Caribbean but proved equally adept at destabilizing them.

Without the decisive advantage that yellow fever conferred upon defenders, the French and especially the Spanish would not have been able to hold their Caribbean possessions against Britain. Certainly the financial and strategic costs of defending the Caribbean from the Royal Navy would have been incalculably higher. And without Havana, Cartagena, Portobello, San Juan, and a few other key points, Spanish power could not assure the safe passage of the treasure fleets from the Americas to Spain, nor could it control, administer, and retain major portions of the Spanish empire. The British apparently had no compunctions about absorbing territories in which foreign colonists resided: the Dutch of South Africa and the French of Quebec found themselves incorporated into the British Empire as a result of wartime conquests. There is no reason to assume that the British would have refrained from doing the same to Cuba and Mexico if the costs of conquest and occupation had not seemed intolerably high. Samuel Johnson's "blasts of pestilence" made for a vastly different world.

The Cartagena Expedition, 1740–1742, and Anglo-American Relations

DOUGLAS EDWARD LEACH

Historians of Anglo-American relations, in their seemingly endless exploration of the underlying causes of the American Revolution, have long been probing the dynamics of colonial society, complex statistics of the American economy, intricacies of provincial politics, and the dense thicket of British imperial administration. One additional topic deserving close scrutiny is Anglo-American military relations prior to 1760, with all the tensions engendered by the presence of British regular forces in the colonies. One thinks immediately, for example, of the nagging problem of naval impressment in the various seaports or of the friction produced whenever redcoats were quartered in a provincial town.

In all such approaches—social, economic, political, administrative, military—the scholar should be concerned with not only the actual details of an episode but also the *impact* upon the attitudes of those involved, or, to put it another way, the effect upon British and American perceptions. Unfavorable perceptions, reinforced by subsequent experience, can be the tinder from which a revolution may be kindled.

One major episode that generated a remarkably high intensity of mutual Anglo-American antagonism as early as 1740–42 was the

43

ill-fated British expedition against the great Spanish base of Cartagena on the northern coast of South America. The main outline of
the story is familiar enough. Britain had gone to war with Spain in
1739 ostensibly, as tradition has it, over a crude bit of auricular
surgery performed without benefit of either clergy or anesthesia.
The ministry, having decided to mount a major offensive operation
in the Caribbean, began to assemble a large fleet and many regiments of regular troops. Supreme naval command was given to Vice
Admiral Edward Vernon; command of the army eventually de-
volved upon Brigadier General Thomas Wentworth. Disagreements
between these two officers, and interservice rivalry in general,
proved to be a serious detriment.

Fairly early in the planning it was decided to call on the North
American colonies to raise a sizable contingent of volunteer troops.
This contingent was raised and did participate in the expedition,
most unhappily as it turned out. Cartagena did not fall to the
British. On the contrary, the amphibious assault failed and the bold
venture had to be given up as a bad job—indeed, a signal failure of
British arms. The sound that most perfectly epitomizes that inglori-
ous failure was not the heady thunder of cannon, but rather, day
after weary day, the pathetic splash of British and American corpses
dumped overboard from the fever-racked ships of the fleet. Only a
sorry remnant of the American contingent survived to return home
with a bitter tale of neglect, discrimination, abuse, disease, and
death.

Albert Harkness, Jr., in an article titled "Americanism and Jenkins' Ear," called attention to the "increasingly articulate distrust
between the Englishmen of Europe and the Englishmen of continental America" arising out of this very experience. He spoke of an
"emergent Americanism," pointing out that "the first general employment of the word ["American"] in the sense in which we define
it seems to have been in this expedition where Englishmen and
colonials upon forced association found each other peculiar."[1] Hark-

[1]Albert Harkness, Jr., "Americanism and Jenkins' Ear," *Mississippi Valley Historical
Review* 37 (1950): 61, 88–89.

ness' insight is, in my view, both correct and valuable, providing a sound base for further exploration.

The unhappy relationship between the British professional military personnel and the American provincials contributed significantly to mutually unfavorable perceptions in a slowly swelling tide of Anglo-American antagonism. In this essay, I shall identify the principal causes of American resentment. First, there was the British bureaucratic failure to provide adequately for the American contingent and for its smooth integration with the entire force. On top of that came the ill-concealed contempt of British officers for the appearance and discipline of the Americans, together with the ill-advised exclusion from the British Council of War of Colonel William Gooch, lieutenant-governor of Virginia and commander of the American contingent. Next came the employment of American troops as burden-bearers and laborers and, worse yet, the abusive treatment of American soldiers drafted against their will for service on board ships of the fleet. Finally, we surely must take notice of the overall failure itself, which meant not only humiliation for all involved but also no plunder and hence no personal enrichment, the very prospect that had led the Americans to volunteer for the expedition in the first place.

In approaching this topic we are fortunate in the richness of sources available in official papers and correspondence as well as in the contemporary American press.[2] It had been apparent from the outset that the ministry had no great confidence in American military leadership. The governors of the eleven participating colonies were authorized to issue commissions only at company level; all staff officers and others of field rank were appointed by the Crown. In addition, the regular army was ordered to provide for each of the

[2]First and foremost are the Colonial Office Papers, in particular CO 5/41, CO 5/42, and CO 318/3, in the Public Record Office, London. Also of help are the Additional Manuscripts 32695–32699 in the British Library. The papers of Admiral Vernon have been ably edited by B. M. Ranft as vol. 99 of the *Publications of the Navy Records Society*. Gooch's private correspondence, unfortunately, is closed, but transcripts of his official correspondence in the Public Record Office are on file in Williamsburg.

provincial companies an experienced lieutenant and a sergeant as a
practical way of raising the expected low level of training and
discipline. The army also agreed to furnish the Americans with
uniforms, tents, weapons, and ammunition and to pay them at the
same rates as regular troops. When the campaign was concluded, the
ministry promised, the Americans would be free to return home,
with transportation provided at royal expense.[3]

Recruiting in the colonies thrived mainly on the glittering prospect of plunder, the astute ministry having let it be known that the
provincial troops would receive their fair portion, down to the
lowliest musket-sloper.[4] Normally, a colonist enlisted to serve under
a particular captain whom he knew, at least by reputation, and was
willing to obey. Few men, if any, considered that they were making
a commitment to the British army as such, and all took very
seriously the king's promise to return them home at the conclusion
of the venture. So, in general, the recruiting went remarkably well.
There was, as one official reported, "a strong Disposition in the
People of these Provinces to engage in the Expedition."[5] Lieutenant-
Governor Clarke of New York quickly identified the reason: "the
expectation of growing rich by the Booty, and by gifts of lands and

[3]CO 318/3, various documents dated January to April 1740 (Crown copyright
reserved). See also CO 5/752, fols. 217–20, 250–52, 353–63; British Library Add.
MS. 32693, fols. 161–68, 32698, fols. 177–78. There is little evidence to suggest that
the infusion of British regular lieutenants and sergeants caused great difficulty but
every reason to believe that it actually did help the raw American troops develop a
military appearance. Benjamin Franklin reported in the *Pennsylvania Gazette* that four
of his colony's companies, "by the Care and Diligence of the British Lieutenants
wherewith they are furnish'd, have made a considerable Progress in the new
Exercise." Leonard W. Labaree et al., eds., *The Papers of Benjamin Franklin* (New
Haven: Yale University Press, 1959–), 2:288. But see also CO 5/41, fols. 250–52.
[4]CO 318/3, Draft of instructions to Cathcart for distributing plunder (In Mr.
Bladen's of July 7, 1740). See also E. B. O'Callaghan and Berthold Fernow, eds.,
Documents Relative to the Colonial History of the State of New York (hereafter cited as
DRNY), 15 vols. (Albany: Weed, Parsons, 1856–87), 6:164–67.
[5]CO 5/41, fols. 215–16. See also CO 5/1337, fols. 230–31 (Colonial Williamsburg
Foundation, Research Center, microfilm from Virginia Colonial Records Project;
Crown copyright reserved).

houses . . ."[6] An observant woman in the same colony, however, added the prophetic warning that if the recruits should be disappointed in their expectations, the British would not again find Americans "soe Readily Disposed to fallow [*sic*] the beat of a drum."[7]

The numerous companies were administratively combined into a single regiment known as Gooch's American Foot. Much larger than the normal British regiment, it was subdivided into four battalions. The thirty-six companies constituting this organization hailed from eleven different colonies, each company fiercely jealous of its own provincial identity and primarily loyal to its own provincial officers. Marching in the ranks were men of extremely diverse backgrounds, among them a considerable number of Irish Catholics, probably some American Indians, and possibly a few free blacks. Certainly the great majority were from the lower class—servants, laborers, sons of small farmers. During the fall of 1740, when reasonably ready, the various companies were embarked in chartered merchant vessels at colonial seaports and carried to Jamaica, where, at Kingston and Port Royal, the great British expeditionary force was assembling.

So off they went, several thousand of them, hot for adventure and plunder. Arriving at Jamaica, a tropical island such as few of them had ever seen, they found the British military bureaucracy almost totally unprepared to receive them. Lacking tents, the American troops were forced to remain quartered on board the transports, subsisting on a meager and monotonous diet scraped from rapidly dwindling shipboard stores, without the fresh vegetables needed for good health. Their officers, venturing ashore in the hope of purchasing fresh provisions for the men with whatever small supplies of cash they might have had in their pockets, were confronted in the

---

[6]*DRNY* 6:164. See also CO 5/41, fols. 223–26; *DRNY* 6:167, 171.

[7]Leo Hershkowitz and Isidore S. Meyer, eds., *The Lee Max Friedman Collection of American Jewish Colonial Correspondence: Letters of the Franks Family (1733–1748)* (Waltham, Mass.: American Jewish Historical Society, 1968), p. 76.

markets with Jamaican hucksters demanding grossly inflated prices.[8] Inevitably the Americans began to sicken, and some died. A Massachusetts company, which had made a good appearance before leaving Boston, was now described as "quite broke up and torn to pieces, and look like another People, quite disheartened."[9] According to another account, the men "lay dying like rotten Sheep," a figure of speech that created vivid imagery in the minds of farmers back home.[10] Grumbling against those deemed responsible for these deplorable conditions—the British high command—became epidemic.[11]

Much of the immediate hardship suffered by Gooch's men might have been remedied if the Americans had had ready access to adequate funds. However, not only was it difficult to purchase needed supplies, but also there was little or no money available for the men's wages. There is no simple answer to the question of who was responsible for the shortage of funds. Two Jamaican merchants, Edward Manning and John Meriwether, had been designated by the ministry to serve as agents for transmitting funds to the army. But when these agents were approached for funds to pay the provincial troops they coolly replied that they lacked authorization. Later John Colebrooke, a British disbursing officer who investigated the problem, made serious allegations of unscrupulous financial dealings against these agents and others, but the charges were not proved. All that the frustrated American officers knew was that somehow they were unable to collect from any responsible official the money so desperately needed.[12]

---

[8]One provincial officer, with something other than vegetables in mind, complained that "you cannot open your Mouth at an Ordinary under 4 to 5s. Sterling a Man." *Boston Weekly News-Letter*, March 12–19, 1740/41.

[9]Ibid.

[10]*Boston Evening-Post*, June 29, 1741.

[11]William A. Foote, "The Pennsylvania Men of the American Regiment," *Pennsylvania Magazine of History and Biography* 87 (1963): 36.

[12]CO 5/41 fols. 253–57, 262–63. Colebrooke's interesting letter to Charles Hamburg Williams, M.P. and paymaster general of the marines, is found in PRO, Admiralty Papers 96/512, fol. 7.

Turning to the other side of the coin, the British professional officers were unfavorably impressed with the general appearance of the American troops. Not atypical was the comment made by one navy captain. "From the first review . . . they were despised," he wrote, adding that the colonial officers were of contemptibly low origin, having been "Blacksmiths, Taylors, Barbers, Shoemakers, and all the Bandity them Colonies affords: insomuch that the other part of the Army [the regulars] held them at Scorn." [13] After having inspected one of Gooch's battalions, General Wentworth reported that "there are amongst 'em very good men, and some exceeding bad; they are very little acquainted with discipline, but if they prove, what they appear to be, men accustomed to fatigue, I am in hopes that they may do good service." [14] The latter part of Wentworth's comment reveals his intention to use the Americans not as combat troops but as laborers. As already mentioned, Gooch was not even accorded the courtesy of a seat on the Council of War, despite the size of his command. [15] In short, before the Americans had been in Jamaica two months, they were soured by the British, and the British by them.

As if that was not enough, the fleet that had come from England was not fully manned, and sickness among the sailors after arrival further diminished the crews. The high command knew the remedy for this problem: according to standard royal instructions, the commanding general was authorized to requisition soldiers for manning the ships—and who more available than the unsoldierly Americans? Groups of dismayed and angry provincial soldiers were soon being separated from their units, conveyed under guard, and dumped on board various ships of war to become sailors. If Gooch protested, he did so in vain. Records indicate that on March 31,

---

[13]CO 5/41, fols. 289, 294; found also in [Charles Knowles], *An Account of the Expedition to Carthagena, with Explanatory Notes and Observations*, 2d ed. (London: n.p., 1743), pp. 38n, 56.

[14]CO 5/42, fols. 26–27. See also CO 5/42, fols. 28–29.

[15]CO 5/41, fols. 264–65; CO 5/42, fols. 54–55. See also CO 5/1337, fols. 254–55 (Colonial Williamsburg Foundation).

1741, as many as 2,479 enlisted men of the American regiment actually were serving in the fleet.[16]

In the meantime, the high command had agreed upon Cartagena, generally believed to be a storehouse of wealth, as the major objective. Its capture would not only undermine Spanish prestige throughout the Western Hemisphere, but also would greatly enrich the victors. When all was in readiness, the great British armada, including the now-scattered American contingent, departed from Jamaica. Arriving near Cartagena early in March 1740/41, the regulars were eventually landed, and soon thereafter some of the American troops together with numbers of black laborers were set to work ashore clearing ground for a camp. Some days later the Council of War recommended that General Wentworth be rein-forced by landing "all such of the American Forces, as he should judge proper to be trusted on shore."[17] The reservation is significant, especially as the general himself remarked that from those American troops "much can not be expected."[18] About a week later, a thousand or more of the Americans were landed in time to participate in the

[16]CO 5/42, fols. 21–22, 32–33, 84–85. The official authorization states that the general may order that the soldiers "shall mann the Ships, where there shall be Occasion for Them, and when They can be spared from the Land Service." Similarly, Vernon had instructions "to order the Sailors, under his Command, to assist Our Land Forces and Marines, and to mann the Batteries, when there may be Occasion for Them, and when They can be spared from the Sea Service." Add. MS 33028, fols. 386–95 (found also in CO 318/3). Such instructions to commanders of joint expeditions were routine. See also the *Boston Weekly News-Letter*, March 12–19, 1740/41; B. M. Ranft, ed., *The Vernon Papers*, Publications of the Navy Records Society, 99 ([London]: Navy Records Society, 1958), pp. 13–14.

[17]Add. MS. 19332, fol. 117. See also Robert Beatson, *Naval and Military Memoirs of Great Britain, from 1727 to 1783*, 6 vols., reprint ed. (Boston: Gregg, 1972), 1:103. The Americans did enjoy some brief moments of glory. On one occasion an assault party of Virginians and sailors dealt effectively with two Spanish batteries that menaced the site of the British camp. At another time, while the leaders of the army were discussing the best way to capture a convent perched on the summit of a strategically located hill, a party of roving Americans made their way up to the convent and soon sent down word that they were in control of the place. *Boston Evening-Post*, June 1, 1741; CO 5/41, fol. 310.

[18]CO 5/42, fols. 30–31.

attack on a Spanish strong point blocking the approach to Cartagena. As expected, the Americans were given an auxiliary assignment as burden-bearers. One group lugged bags of grenades. Another carried scaling ladders, while yet others bore wool packs, shovels, and mattocks. For a number of reasons the attack failed miserably. The British noted the unsoldierlike performance of Gooch's men. Wrote Wentworth to the duke of Newcastle: "What much added to our Misfortune was the wretched Behaviour of the Americans, who had the Charge of the Scaling Ladders, working Tools, etc., which they threw down on the first Approach of Danger, and thereby occasioned the loss of the greatest part of 'em."[19]

Thereafter, problems of camp and ship were more destructive than the enemy. Water was in short supply; epidemic disease intensified; graves proliferated. At last the British high command, beset by internal controversy, recognized the futility of further effort and ordered reembarkation. On board the ships during the ensuing days when Vernon lingered off the coast, and during the return voyage to Jamaica, conditions were appalling. One Briton wrote to his brother in London, "We are in a Mesirable [*sic*] condition for want of fresh provision, our meet is salt as brine, our bread as it lays on the table swarms with Maggots, and the water here fluxes us all."[20] By the time the fleet returned to Port Royal, Wentworth's army, including the bedraggled American regiment, was greatly reduced, as were the crews of Vernon's ships. The *Boston Weekly News-Letter* for July 30–August 6, 1741, reported that in one Massachusetts company twenty-three men had perished before the return from Cartagena, and twenty-five men plus an ensign since, for a casualty rate of about 50 percent.

Then a field-grade vacancy occurred in the American regiment. Instead of promoting one of the provincial captains, Wentworth gave the post to a non-American officer even though his commission

[19]CO 5/42, fols. 35–38. See also CO 5/41, fol. 314, and Beatson, *Naval and Military Memoirs*, 1:105–06.
[20]Add. MS. 34207, fols. 9–11.

was of more recent date. "Whatever Reasons the General may have for not Promoting any of the American Captains I am a stranger to them," Gooch complained to the secretary of state. "I could not prevail with him to Advance any of my Own."[21] Here is an early example of a cause of dispute that became intense during the subsequent war: British insistence that a royal commission, regardless of date, took precedence over a commission issued by a colonial governor.

And now, what of the promised return home? Once again the admiral followed the practice of drafting soldiers from Gooch's regiment to help man the ships. Such duty, the Americans realized, would lessen the possibility of early discharge and might even involve a long voyage to another part of the world. But when Vernon demanded men and Wentworth acquiesced, there was no practical way for Gooch or any other officer to stop them. By the end of May 1741, according to one report, most of the chartered vessels that had brought Gooch's companies from North America had been given clearance for the return voyage, but, unfortunately, the majority of the surviving provincial troops who yearned to sail on them were dispersed among ships of the Royal Navy.[22] These American troops were supposedly assigned only temporarily to duty with the fleet, and not formally pressed into the navy, but the distinction meant little so long as they were retained on board ship.

There is strong evidence that these unfortunates were subjected to harsh treatment that extended, in some cases, to systematic abuse. One may surmise that British naval personnel had remarkably low

[21]CO 5/1337, fols. 254–55 (Colonial Williamsburg Foundation).

[22]*Boston Weekly News-Letter*, June 25–July 2, 1741. Thirteen American soldiers in particular had reason to feel victimized. They were enjoying themselves ashore, not in proper uniform, when one of Vernon's press gangs pounced upon them and, despite their protests, hauled them away for naval service. Later, when word of this action reached officers of the American regiment, an unsuccessful attempt was made to have the soldiers returned to their units. In this case, involving actual impressment, even Wentworth was helpless. Eventually the ministry properly ordered the men sent back to their regiment. Add. MS. 32698, fols. 175–78. See also CO 5/42, fols. 97–98, 104–07, 188–89.

tolerance for Americans, especially those so audacious as to assert their rights. Notable cases of abuse are described in a memorial dated February 3, 1742, and addressed to Wentworth by field officers of Gooch's regiment.[23] It contains only allegations, but there is little likelihood that those officers would have endorsed the complaints without first being convinced that the abuse was serious. Drafts of American soldiers had been distributed among ships of the fleet, often unaccompanied by their own officers. When HMS *Dunkirk*, for example, departed for England she had on board fifty-two Americans from sixteen different companies. Wentworth himself verified this complaint when he asserted that Vernon did not hesitate to move soldiers from ship to ship, "by which means, there are frequently, men without officers and officers without men . . ."[24]

Captain Park Pepper of the American regiment testified that "he was several months on board the Rippon man of War on duty, with a Detachment of Sixty five Americans, that he had frequent Complaints made by his men of the ill treatment they received on board, but was never able to relieve them, tho' frequently represented to the Officers of the Ship." In particular he cited "the cruel usage Samuel Wilson of Capt Bushrods Company received from one Slaughter a midshipman . . . by beating and kicking said Wilson in so barbarous a manner 'twas supposed he would have died." Wilson subsequently did die. One of Pepper's own men was "kept working at the Chain pump five Glasses Successively on board the Prince Frederick, tho' it was customary to relieve every hour, and in the running of the five glasses was so unmercifully beaten by Lieut Hughes of said Ship . . . whilst naked at his Work that he was cutt into the side the mark whereof is very visible." Some of the American soldiers said that they "had rather die than undergo such usage any longer."[25] Wentworth himself, siding with the Americans against Vernon, wrote that "the Gentlemen of the Sea, especially

[23]CO 5/42, fols. 190–91. See also CO 5/1337, fols. 256–57 (Colonial Williamsburg Foundation).
[24]CO 5/42, fols. 164–65.
[25]CO 5/42, fols. 190–91.

the Warrant Officers, do not spare to exert their Authority";[26] and on July 22, 1742, he engaged in a heated argument with Vernon as to whether soldiers temporarily on shipboard duty were subject to army or navy discipline.[27]

Such abuses continued month after month, while the list of American dead grew ever longer. Survivors wondered when, if ever, the British high command would honor the promise under which they had enlisted. At long last, on August 5, 1742, approximately sixteen months after the futile attempt against Cartagena, the ministry ordered Vernon and Wentworth to dissolve the expedition, send home Gooch's American Foot, and return to England. These orders contain a tone of serious misgiving about the way the Americans had been treated, with special regard to the potentially harmful effect whenever Britain again found need to call for colonial recruits. That this apprehension was realistic was clearly indicated almost four years later, when Britain was attempting to raise an American expedition against Canada. In a letter of June 13, 1746, written to the secretary of state by one of the disgruntled survivors of the Cartagena expedition, Lieutenant-Governor William Gooch himself, expressed his view that it might not be easy to persuade American colonists to enlist for the new venture, "especially, if, as I am told, we are not to expect any of those men, who were on the last Expedition, they not having digested the hard Usage of being Broke in Jamaica, and sent Home without a farthing in their Pockets."[28]

The American regiment was officially disbanded October 24, 1742, leaving considerable numbers of its men in hospital at Jamaica, or in garrison elsewhere, or scattered among the fleet. How many of the approximately 3,500 who originally went to the Caribbean actually survived to reach home is difficult to determine, but the

---

[26]CO 5/42, fols. 164–65.

[27]CO 5/42, fols. 242–46.

[28]CO 5/1338, fols. 6–7, 11–12 (Colonial Williamsburg Foundation). I am grateful to Dr. John Hemphill of the Colonial Williamsburg Foundation for bringing this transcript to my attention.

number cannot have been more than a pathetic fraction of the total.[29] Those who did return seem to have slipped quietly back into the populace of the colonies, having brought home no glory and no riches, only bitter memories. They had not been very effective soldiers or very good sailors. Their motives for joining the expedition had been less patriotic than mercenary. So they came back badly disillusioned, to spread among their acquaintances their vivid recollections of British callousness, interservice quarreling, confusion and inefficiency at all levels, and a general atmosphere of incompetence and failure. At the same time, British professional military personnel who had served with the Americans in the Caribbean were bringing back to their colleagues and countrymen further support for the hardening impression that provincial troops were stubbornly averse to discipline and were cowardly in battle.

Britons and colonists alike were beginning to sense more clearly than ever the emergence of significant differences between the two peoples. The great Cartagena expedition of 1740–42 contributed heavily not only to the mutually antagonistic views of British regulars and American provincials, which had been developing for many years, but also to the emergence of a self-conscious Americanism with almost incalculable import for the British Empire.

[29]Add. MS. 32699, fols. 350–54, 359–64. During the summer of 1741 some members of the American regiment participated in a futile British invasion of Cuba. The following year a group of volunteers from the same regiment, lured no doubt by a lingering hope of material gain, was involved in a British project for colonizing the island of Roatán off the coast of Honduras. Periodic muster returns for the American regiment, giving some idea of losses, may be found in CO 5/42.

The Adaptation of
the British Army to
Wilderness Warfare, 1755–1763

DANIEL J. BEATTIE

In 1755, the year of the disastrous Braddock expedition to the Forks of the Ohio, a young British officer, newly arrived in America, wrote home, "I cannot conceive how war can be made in such a country."[1] The problems involved in campaigning in North America that confronted British commanders were formidable indeed. The basic military challenges of strategy and tactics, logistics and administration were present, of course. British generals had learned these elements of military science and art and had seen them practiced in Europe. The books and treatises on such subjects that they read were based on European models. Such skills would be needed in the conflict that would culminate in the conquest of Canada. But American conditions would demand change in the European practice of war in several important respects.

Probably the greatest difficulties for commanders were posed by the vastness of the theater of operations. New England was larger than old England. In fact, England was only a bit larger than the Crown Colony of New York (including the lands of the Iroquois). A commander might have to control and supply forces separated by

---

[1] Lee McCardell, *Ill-Starred General: Braddock of the Coldstream Guards* (Pittsburgh: University of Pittsburgh Press, 1958), p. 180.

many hundreds of miles. The British Isles, the source of reinforcements, some supplies, and orders, was an ocean away. Furthermore, most of the area of campaigning was a virtually trackless and uninhabited wilderness. The frontier regions of New York, Pennsylvania, or Nova Scotia were not like Flanders, Hanover, Silesia, or Italy. As Francis Parkman long ago pointed out, the real adversary of British commanders was the wilderness itself: having conquered it, they would find defeating the whitecoats in battle a comparatively easy task.[2] But there were plenty of other problems in America besides distance and ruggedness of terrain. Among them were: Indian relations, aid from the provincials, coordination of operations with the Royal Navy, extra opportunities for desertion, local procurement of recruits and provisions, and maintenance of army discipline and health. All of these problems and others are closely related to the central question of how to move troops and supplies across a wilderness, how to operate in a non-European environment.

British leaders were not obtuse. They recognized the central problem early on; but like their descendants in World War I who wrestled with stalemate on the western front (the conundrum of overcoming trenches, machine guns, and artillery), they were not successful immediately. The forest beat many a commander between 1755 and 1763. The difficulties of campaigning in a wilderness explain in part the long string of British failures in the French and Indian War. Yet the degree to which the British army and its leaders adapted to the American environment explains in part why the years of frustration were eventually followed by the years of triumph.

Many of the stereotypes of the British army in America derive from the Braddock campaign of 1755. Supposedly Braddock was a fool, unwilling to adapt to American conditions. He attempted to apply parade-ground maneuvers to a march across the wilderness and stupidly forced his men to fight in the European manner in

---

[2]Francis Parkman, *Montcalm and Wolfe*, 2 vols. (Boston: Little, Brown, 1911–12).

terrain utterly unsuited to such tactics.[3] This view of Braddock and his expedition is nonsense. The Newcastle ministry sent Braddock and two regiments to the New World to gain possession of the Forks of the Ohio and oust French trespassers elsewhere along the border between the British colonies and New France. As soon as he landed in Virginia, Braddock acted with vigor and skill to prepare an expedition. He was furious at the difficulties he encountered with penny-pinching colonial assemblies and crooked contractors. Fortunately, he finally obtained the crucial wagons and drivers he needed through the help of Benjamin Franklin. The Crown also sent with him two understrength regiments from Ireland. Their ranks were filled with "drafts" from other units—in other words, those soldiers undesired by their parent battalions. In America, poor-quality American recruits joined to increase each regiment's strength by 50 percent. Braddock drilled them hard, but they were far from being highly disciplined, well-trained, and tightly knit units when they began their march to the Forks of the Ohio.[4]

Braddock recognized that his force might well be attacked by enemy irregulars. He trained his troops in march security, created a second grenadier company in each battalion, lightened the gear that

[3]For example, a widely used American history college text: "Brave but aged, wise in the ways of European warfare but unused to the American woods, Braddock wore out his men by having them cut a long military road through the forest to Fort Duquesne, and he exposed them to attack from the tree-hidden enemy by marching them in the accepted European formation. Seven miles from the fort he ran into a French and Indian ambush." Richard Current, T. Harry Williams, and Frank Freidel, *American History: A Survey*, 4th ed. (New York: Alfred A. Knopf, 1975).

[4]On the Braddock campaign, see: Lawrence H. Gipson, *The British Empire Before the American Revolution*, 10 vols. (New York: Alfred A. Knopf, 1946–70), vol. 6: *The Years of Defeat*; Paul E. Kopperman, *Braddock at the Monongahela* (Pittsburgh: University of Pittsburgh Press, 1976); McCardell, *Ill-Starred General*; Parkman, *Montcalm and Wolfe*; and Stanley Pargellis, ed., *Military Affairs in North America, 1748–1765, Selected Documents from the Cumberland Papers in Windsor Castle* (New York: D. Appleton-Century, for the American Historical Association, 1936). The best general works on the French and Indian Wars are Gipson, *British Empire*; Parkman, *Montcalm and Wolfe*; Pargellis, *Military Affairs*; and Douglas E. Leach, *Arms for Empire: A Military History of the British Colonies in North America, 1607–1763* (New York: Macmillan, 1973).

each soldier had to carry, and attempted to secure provincial back-woodsmen and Indians for the expedition. He could not see how undisciplined savages could be a threat to his army; he did perceive their usefulness as scouts. Only a few Indians could be persuaded to join him, however, and few stayed very long.

The general discovered that his instructions were confused and their designers ignorant of geography. He was ordered to take an unnecessarily arduous route to Fort Duquesne. His maps were grossly inaccurate.[5] He was supposed to lead an army over fifteen miles of wilderness when the reality was more than a hundred miles. It is no wonder he considered forgetting the whole thing.[6]

For a month his army marched toward its goal and built a military road as it went. The French at Duquesne looked for an opportunity to attack, but Braddock and his 2,500 men were ever on guard.[7] That is, they kept up their guard in the manner of a European army until they were close to their object. With the French fort just ahead, the redcoats began to think their enemies had retreated without a fight. They relaxed their guard—then the French and Indians struck them.

Braddock's defeat was not an ambush: the two forces collided. For two hours the British soldiers, eventually nearly encircled, fired through the smoke into the trees. They ignored the orders of some of their officers to use cold steel in the European manner. Overconfidence had been replaced by confusion and panic, and in the end they ran. The retreat was protected by Virginia provincials under George Washington, who heard the dying Braddock's assertion that the British would do better next time.[8]

[5]Pargellis, *Military Affairs*, pp. 82, 85.

[6]Winthrop Sargent, ed., *A History of the Expedition Against Fort Duquesne, in 1755 Under General Edward Braddock* (Philadelphia: Historical Society of Pennsylvania, 1855), pp. 16ff.

[7]Pargellis, *Military Affairs*, pp. 129ff.

[8]Benjamin Franklin, *Autobiography*, ed. Frank Pine (New York: Garden City, 1916), p. 268.

Another expedition of 1755 was stillborn. Governor William
Shirley of Massachusetts aimed to attack Niagara with two regiments just recruited in the colonies. He lacked organizational skill,
and his hired boatmen and provincial troops grumbled at the
back-breaking toil of pulling themselves and their supplies up the
Mohawk River Valley. Shirley was slowed and was finally halted at
Oswego by the season of storms. The expedition was disbanded
except for the two new regiments of redcoats who were left in a new
fort at Oswego. Ill-trained, ill-equipped, ill-fed, and sickly, these
two regiments would be captured en masse by the French the next
summer. Elsewhere in New York Colony, William Johnson led a
little army of psalm-singing New Englanders toward Lake George.
A stronger army of French regulars, Canadians, and Indians
pounced upon him; but he shattered their assaults and drove them
off. Because his provincials had had enough of war, he had to give
up any hope of capturing the French fort at St. Frédéric (Crown
Point). Only in Nova Scotia did one British offensive of 1755 bear
fruit: General Robert Monckton captured Fort Beauséjour. Meanwhile, from the Shenandoah Valley to the Upper Connecticut, a red
sea of murder inundated the frontier as French and Indians ravaged
the farms and settlements of the backcountry.[9]

Shirley, now commander in chief of His Majesty's forces in North
America, had few dependable forces to use in 1756. That year the
frontiers were again aflame, Oswego fell, and the British government replaced Shirley with the earl of Loudoun and more regulars.
Loudoun did not last long. In 1757 he attempted to capture Fortress
Louisbourg, the French Gibraltar of North America. Louisbourg
guarded the entrance to the St. Lawrence and the French fisheries
off the Grand Banks. For this expedition, Loudoun had over 14,000
redcoats and thirty-three warships. The French advantages, in
addition to their garrison at Louisbourg, included the wretched
climate of Cape Breton Island and Nova Scotia and the indecision of
Loudoun himself.

[9]The most complete and most dry account of the campaigns of this war is Gipson,
British Empire.

The British experienced yet another terrible year in 1757. Loudoun gave up before the stronghold of Louisbourg. The French seized Fort William Henry on Lake George and massacred part of its garrison of redcoats and provincials. The frontier of the British colonies was again pushed eastward by Indian raiders. Loudoun was replaced with General James Abercromby.

The next year, 1758, would see the last of the great disasters to British armies in the war and two great victories. Abercromby sent his fine army, the largest in the war, to a suicidal assault on the French Fort Carillon at Ticonderoga. But General John Forbes took possession of the Forks of the Ohio by the end of the year. Forbes' campaign against Fort Duquesne was even more systematic and slower than that of Braddock. With only a regiment and a half of regulars and 4,000 provincials, he built a road to victory. He discovered too that the wilderness was his main foe. Instead of following Braddock's route, he approached the forks by way of Pennsylvania. He ordered his capable assistant, Lieutenant General Henry Bouquet, to build a road westward, a road connecting fortified supply depots in the European manner. Forbes assembled his army and supplies in Philadelphia as Bouquet constructed the road. The French-led Indians grew discouraged and deserted their allies after failing to capture one of Bouquet's tough little forts. Before the end of the year, the Forks of the Ohio were British.

Jeffery Amherst, a new general picked by William Pitt for energy and intelligence, was assigned to take Louisbourg in 1758. He worked closely with the Royal Navy in the campaign and successfully landed his army on a well-defended coast, besieged Louisbourg and captured it.[10] Amherst was promoted after Louisbourg to overall command in America; his able subordinate James Wolfe became the leader of an expedition against Quebec in 1759.

Over the preceding three years the British army in America had developed a sound logistical and transport system to cope with American conditions. The army also had experimented with various

---

[10]For Louisbourg, see J. S. McLennan, *Louisbourg, from its Foundation to its Fall* (Sydney, Nova Scotia: Fortress, 1969).

types of light infantry—irregular and regular—to enable it to counter the French and Indians. Together these two developments, the logistical system and the use of light infantry, mark how well England's army had adjusted to wilderness campaigning in North America. The army that Jeffery Amherst led in 1759 and 1760 had acquired skills that allowed it to overcome its primary obstacles: distance and the American wilderness.

The greatest accomplishment of the cautious Loudoun was to put army supply and transport on a sound footing. Before he left England, Loudoun had conferred with the duke of Cumberland, Henry Fox, and the earl of Halifax about the failure of the Oswego campaign of 1755.[11] A faulty supply system seemed most to blame. Accordingly, the ministry decided to place contracting for North America in the hands of three prosperous London merchants, Sir William Baker, Christopher Kilby, and Richard Baker. William Baker was supplying satisfactorily most of the troops in Nova Scotia, and Kilby had lived in Connecticut. The Crown signed a twelve-month, renewable contract with the firm of Baker, Kilby, and Baker on March 26, 1756; and on April 1, 1756, the firm began to operate.[12] By the terms of the contract one of the partners was to handle matters in America, where many of the provisions would be procured. As security, the firm deposited £100,000 in London. In North America, the commander in chief set up several centrally located Crown storehouses. The contractors were obliged to have at all times enough provisions in these storehouses to support at least 12,000 men for six months. The provisions were to be wholesome, and the commander in chief would appoint inspectors under a commissary of stores and provisions to verify the contents of the storehouses. Unsuitable provisions were to be replaced immediately at the contractors' expense. The firm would submit receipts for transportation expenses to the commissary of stores for reim-

[11]Stanley Pargellis, *Lord Loudoun in North America* (New Haven: Yale University Press, 1933), p. 67.

[12]Text of the contract: War Office 34 (Amherst Papers; hereafter cited as WO), vol. 69.

bursement, and the Treasury in London would make monthly payments to the firm on the basis of certificates endorsed by the commander in chief and the commissary. The firm was paid six-pence per day per man fed, which would provide each private man a "ration" or one-seventh of the weekly allowance of "seven pounds of beef, or in lieu thereof, four pounds of pork, which is thought to be equivalent; seven pounds of biscuit bread, or the same weight of flour, six ounces of butter, three pints of pease, [and] half a pound of rice . . ."[13]

This system, with its main storehouses at New York, Albany, and Halifax, functioned well throughout the war, although the firm of Baker, Kilby, and Baker was replaced by another in 1760. Salted meat, peas, and butter generally came from Ireland and England. The other staples, as well as fresh meat, which was issued to the sick and for two days per week in winter to everyone, were obtained in the "provision colonies."[14] Christopher Kilby was honest and hardworking and had agents in every large town and seaport. On September 3, 1758, he wrote Abercromby that the need for fresh pork "drove our searches thro't all the Neighboring Colonies and the back Countrys in pursuit of a supply."[15] But even Connecticut—the "Pork Colony"—was barren. In his search for fresh meat and vegetables for the winter garrisons, Kilby discovered "from my own Experience throughout the Continent no one Individual has yet been found that can be depended for any Certain & Constant Supply of Provisions, for anytime or at any place."[16]

Robert Leake, commissary of stores and provisions, was an astute and suspicious guardian of the king's interests.[17] He was aided in part by young provincial gentlemen like Philip Schuyler, who were

---

[13]John Knox, *An Historical Journal of the Campaigns in North America . . . (1769)*, 3 vols., ed. Arthur G. Doughty (Toronto: Champlain Society, 1914), 1:1.

[14]The Middle Atlantic colonies.

[15]Christopher Kilby to James Abercromby, September 3, 1758, WO 34, vol. 69.

[16]Ibid.

[17]Leake was perhaps too suspicious. In 1757, Kilby proved that many of the provisions condemned by Leake were fit. Pargellis, *Lord Loudoun*, p. 295.

"of the posture" (i.e., high society) and who were lured by large salaries into serving the regulars as contractors of provisions on the theory that they were less prone to graft. All of this organization involved large responsibilities and big money. In 1756 and 1757 the firm of Baker, Kilby, and Baker supplied five million rations and was paid £123,409 11s. 10d. In 1758 they were paid £215,150 10s. 6d. because large numbers of provincials were fed that year.[18]

This supply organization could not have been successful without an efficient transport system. Loudoun created the efficient transport that paved the way to victory for Amherst. Two situations were involved—transport overland and transport by water. In both cases dependability and honesty were required, and not often found, among the provincials who offered their services to the army. Wagons and carts were rented, along with their drivers, to work by the day and distance. Even if dependable wagoners were obtained, cartage was extremely expensive. In 1756 shipping barrels from Albany to Lake George cost nearly half the value of their contents of food.[19] The remedy was the establishment of a Crown-owned wagon corps, the first of its kind in the British army and one not duplicated until the Napoleonic Wars.[20]

Captain Gabriel Christie, assistant deputy quartermaster general, suggested the idea, and Loudoun accepted it in early 1757. The army built a wagon barn and stables at Albany. Fifty wagons and

[18]Ibid., p. 292.
[19]Ibid., p. 297.
[20]Colonel R. H. Beadon, *The Royal Army Service Corps, a History of Transport and Supply in the British Army*, 2 vols. (Cambridge: Cambridge University Press, 1931), is deficient for the eighteenth century. George C. Shaw, *Supply in Modern War* (London: Faber and Faber, 1938), is archaic but interesting. Of greater application is Michael Glover's superb book, *Peninsula Preparation: The Reform of the British Army, 1795–1809* (Cambridge: Cambridge University Press, 1963), which has chapters on supply, administration, training, and other vital functions of the army. King Lawrence Parker, "Anglo-American Wilderness Campaigning 1754–1764: Logistical and Tactical Developments" (Ph.D. diss., Columbia University, 1970), is interesting. Recent, provocative, but covering this period only briefly (pp. 26–39), is Martin Van Creveld, *Supplying War: Logistics from Wallenstein to Patton* (Cambridge: Cambridge University Press, 1977).

110 horses were bought, and regular regiments supplied volunteers as drivers. The final establishment of the wagon corps was a director, subdirector, two assistants, and fifty drivers. Loudoun estimated that the Crown saved £3,400 over one six-month period by having its own wagon train.[21] He also hired ninety ox teams from Connecticut. Oxen were slower than horses, but they could pull heavier loads and were hardier. Loudoun also made a major effort to standardize the army's boats. Hitherto, transport boats came in various sizes and shapes, making packing and transport subject to the disparate sizes of the available vessels. Now the size of scows was standardized to thirty-eight by twelve feet, with a crew of five, and capable of carrying sixty barrels weighing thirty pounds each. Bateaux were to carry 1,500 pounds per vessel of twenty-five to thirty feet in length.[22]

Lieutenant Colonel John Bradstreet, deputy quartermaster general, was in charge of this standardization as well as general supervision of transport for the army. He had held the position since the time of Shirley's command.[23] Shirley's inability to supervise logistical details or pick competent subordinates to do so had produced many errors; but one brilliant exception had been his choice in March 1756 of Major John Bradstreet to lead a corps of armed boatmen. Bradstreet had been lieutenant-governor of St. Johns, Newfoundland; he knew how to handle provincials and how to master wilderness campaigning. He was Shirley's adjutant general, and Shirley felt he was just the man to organize the transportation of

[21]Loudoun Papers, Henry E. Huntington Library, 1723 and 3214.

[22]Ibid., 1342. See the Francis Parkman Papers, Massachusetts Historical Society, no. 43, p. 30, for the sizes of British bateaux. A large bateau carried two barrels of salt pork, four barrels of flour, one barrel of peas, one firkin of butter, and one barrel of rum as a standard load. The barrels were of various sizes, according to the items they held. The weight of the provisions was 1,732 pounds. Loudoun Papers, 1342.

[23]Sir John St. Clair was the deputy quartermaster general in America from 1755 to 1757. Major James Robertson held the position temporarily from March to December 1757, when Bradstreet assumed the title. A quartermaster general was in overall control of supplying the army with provisions, arranging for quarters, and organizing troop movements. "Deputy" was the highest title for the role given in North America.

supplies. He was now ordered to raise forty companies of armed bateauxmen who could move supplies expeditiously across the wilderness and defend themselves if attacked. Each company had fifty men. A company of carpenters was also formed to cut away obstructions on the Mohawk River and Wood Creek. By the early summer of 1756, Bradstreet's American boatmen were bringing supplies regularly to Oswego; they also proved that they could defend themselves. The French and Indians, nine hundred strong, set an ambush on the Onondaga River, nine miles from Oswego, for a convoy of provisions led by Bradstreet in July 1756. Bradstreet took direct command once the fight began and, after several hours of indecisive Indian-style fighting behind trees, led his men in an assault on the enemy. The charge routed the French and Indians. Frontier skirmishing prevented disaster, but Bradstreet's European-style bayonet attack brought victory. But even with such a conscientious, intelligent, and skilled soldier as fiery-tempered Bradstreet in control, many things could go wrong on a long supply route.

Sloops carried matériel from New York City to Albany. Twelve miles above Albany was the key transit point of Half Moon, where everything being sent up the Hudson and Mohawk rivers had to be shifted to land carriage.[24] If the barrels were being sent westward, wagons would haul them to Schenectady, where they would be transferred to bateaux for the journey up the Mohawk River. The trip to Oswego involved numerous portages where the boats and their loads were carried, or pushed across log rollers, to deep water. Northward from Half Moon, wagons hauled provisions and stores over a bad woodland road that crossed numerous ravines over rickety bridges before reaching the hamlet of Stillwater, twelve miles away. A usually muddy track led to Saratoga, five miles distant, but it was customary to use scows in the Hudson to reach that settlement. Wagons or ox carts were used between Saratoga and

---

[24]The Hudson had rifts about Half Moon. Cohoes Falls, with "the roar of a Storm at Sea heard from the Land in the dead of Night," near the mouth of the Mohawk, made a portage necessary. The quotation is from Thomas Pownall, *A Topographical Decription of Such Parts of North America* . . . (London: J. Almon, 1776), p. 35.

Fort Edward, a distance of fifteen miles, and between Fort Edward and the shore of Lake George, another sixteen miles.[25] The obstacles included bad weather, equipment failures, the enemy, and human carelessness. Even if nothing extraordinary happened, it was a slow trek. At the beginning of 1758, Abercromby asked Bradstreet how long it would take to supply the twenty thousand provincials that he expected would gather at Lake George. Bradstreet answered precisely that the optimal time of transport would be three weeks, moving 5,760 barrels in a thousand bateaux, eight hundred wagons, and a thousand ox carts.[26]

It was extremely important to educate officers and civilians to the care that must be taken in transporting supplies and military stores. More than once, provisions were left to spoil in the open or in inadequate lean-tos at Schenectady, Stillwater, Saratoga, and Fort Edward. In September 1757 General Webb found a thousand barrels of flour at Saratoga ruined through exposure. Two hundred and fifty barrels were judged fit—they had only about ten pounds of mildewed flour mixed in with good flour.[27]

Loudoun and Bradstreet did much to systematize the logistical "tail" of the army; equally significant were the steps Shirley, Loudoun, and others took to find the keenest "eyes" for the British forces. By the end of 1758, John Bradstreet's dedication had resulted in a well-fed and supplied British army in America. Robert Rogers's daring was giving British commanders more knowledge of the enemy than ever before. To many British officers, America was "an immense uninhabited Wilderness overgrown everywhere with trees . . . and underbrush, so that no where can anyone see twenty

[25]Loudoun Papers, 4371, gives a good description of this route in 1757. Twenty thousand pounds of provisions were needed to feed a battalion of a thousand men for one week. Eleven or twelve bateaux and twice as many wagons were required to convey this amount from Albany to Lake George. The trip took six days. Loudoun Papers, 2549.

[26]Pargellis, *Lord Loudoun*, pp. 298–99.

[27]Loudoun Papers, 4397.

yards."[28] Since "la petite guerre" was common in the American forest, British commanders followed the example of their European counterparts and looked to local inhabitants for irregular auxiliaries. But British generals were disappointed in the skirmishing abilities of Indians and provincials. They discovered that Indians were expert woodsmen but also that they were not amenable to the lightest discipline. Neither side in the war wanted the Indians as enemies, but as allies they practically had to be left to their own devices, for they could not easily be restrained. And the British believed Indians were devastated by liquor—"dissolute, enfeebled, and indolent when sober, and intractable and mischievous in the Liquour, always quarreling, and often murdering one another."[29] Indians could be used as minor auxiliaries, or better, to teach whites woodland warfare, as the duke of Cumberland recommended.[30]

Recourse was next made to frontiersmen, who might be hired to scout and to skirmish for the regulars. Gorham's rangers had been raised as early as 1750 in Nova Scotia, and they were still active.[31] But they were needed where they were, and Governor Shirley

---

[28]General John Forbes, *Writings of General John Forbes, Relating to His Service in North America* (Menasha, Wis.: Collegiate, 1938), p. 123.

[29]Benjamin Franklin, *A Treaty held with the Ohio Indians, at Carlisle, In October, 1753,* in *The Papers of Benjamin Franklin,* ed. Leonard W. Labaree (New Haven: Yale University Press, 1959–), 5:107.

[30]Cumberland to Loudoun, October 22, 1756, in Pargellis, *Military Affairs,* p. 251. On the Indians, see: Wendell S. Hadlock, "War Among the Northeastern Woodland Indians," *American Anthropologist,* n.s., 49 (1947): 204–21; John Mahon, "Anglo-American Methods of Indian Warfare, 1676–1794," *Mississippi Valley Historical Review* 45 (1958–59): 254–75; John Tebbel and Keith Jennison, *The American Indian Wars* (New York: Harper Brothers, 1960); Harry Turney-High, *Primitive War* (Columbia: University of South Carolina Press, 1949); and Daniel E. Worcester, "The Weapons of American Indians," *New Mexico Historical Review* 20 (1945): 227–38.

[31]Joseph Gorham's rangers served the Crown until 1765. They were later known as the "North American Rangers" and served at Quebec in 1759 and 1760, at Havana in 1762, and at Detroit in 1763. In 1761 Gorham became the only American ranger officer to be awarded a regular commission. Joseph Gorham's father had led a ranger company in Nova Scotia from 1744 to 1750.

looked to the frontiersmen of New Hampshire and New York to help him in 1755.[32] One of them, Robert Rogers, a man bred to the woods, became their most effective leader and eventually commanded "His Majesty's Independent Companies of Rangers."[33] Rogers's rangers seemed for a time to blend the woodsmanship and endurance of the Indians with the discipline and dedication of more civilized soldiers. Soon after he replaced Shirley, Loudoun considered obtaining as many rangers as he could: "It is impossible for an Army to Act in this Country, without *Rangers;* and there ought to be a considerable body of them, and the breeding them up to that, will be a great advantage to the Country, for they will be able to deal with Indians in their own way."[34]

Rogers assumed command of four ranger companies at Fort Edward at the end of 1756. Soon he became the nemesis of the French partisans on the Champlain frontier in summer and in winter. The Champlain–Hudson River Valley system was a chain of river and lakes that lay like a dagger, double-pointed to strike at the heart of either Canada or New York. Its waterways were crucial for both the transport of matériel and the movement of raiders and

[32]William Shirley, *Correspondence of William Shirley, Governor of Massachusetts and Military Commander of North America, 1731–1760,* ed. Charles H. Lincoln (New York: Macmillan, 1912), pp. 453–59. Robert Rogers, *Journals of Major Robert Rogers . . . ,* ed. Franklin B. Hough (Albany: J. Munsell's Sons, 1883), pp. 14–15.

[33]The best written, if biased, account of Rogers's life is John R. Cuneo, *Robert Rogers of the Rangers* (New York: Oxford University Press, 1959). A more detailed account is in Burt B. Loescher, *The History of Rogers' Rangers: The Beginnings, 1755–1758* (San Francisco: Burt B. Loescher, 1949), and in idem, *Genesis, Rogers' Rangers . . . 1758–1783* (San Mateo: Burt B. Loescher, 1969). Rogers's journals are valuable and literate and contain his famous maxims for ranger warfare. Refer also to "Joshua Goodenough's Old Letter," ed. Frederic Remington, in *Harper's New Monthly Magazine* 95 (1897): 878–89, for a personal account of ranger life and prints of the rangers by Remington. Goodenough writes at one point (p. 880): "they would always fight well enough, though often to no good purpose, which was not their fault so much as the headstrong leadership which persisted in making them come to close quarters while at a disadvantage."

[34]Loudoun to Cumberland, November 22, 1756, in Pargellis, *Military Affairs,* p. 269.

regulars. But water routes froze solid in winter, and even though individuals could move on snowshoes and supplies could move on sleds to some extent, major military operations ceased between October and May. As in Europe, there was a definite campaign season of hard ground and warm weather. The regulars went into winter quarters in frontier posts or in towns nearer the coast while the provincial rangers based at Fort Edward harassed and observed the French.

Loudoun had second thoughts about the rangers in 1757: they were extremely expensive, and they were not even regulars.[35] Loudoun was apparently attentive to the advice of Cumberland: "'till *Regular* Officers with men they can trust, learn to beat the woods, & act as *Irregulars*, you will never gain any certain intelligence of the *Enemy*, as I fear, by this time, you are convinced that *Indian* intelligence and that of the *Rangers* is not at all to be depended upon."[36]

When he returned from Louisbourg, Loudoun was determined to convert two companies of each battalion into rangers and possibly to form a separate corps. He invited "gentlemen volunteers" from the regulars to accompany Rogers on his forays and to learn ranging from a master. This plan lasted only two months. The regulars were then ordered back to their units, for Loudoun had discovered another alternative.[37]

Loudoun now decided to form a regular regiment of light infantry. It was the first instance of this in the British army, which, compared to the other European powers, had been tardy in creating regular light infantry to assist and complement the regular battalions. Prussia had its *jaegers* and *freikorps*, Austria its *pandours* and

[35]Pargellis, *Lord Loudoun*, p. 303.
[36]Cumberland to Loudoun, December 2, 1756, in Pargellis, *Military Affairs*, pp. 255–56.
[37]Pargellis, *Lord Loudoun*, pp. 304–05.

grenzer, and France its *chasseurs.*[38] The opening move was made by ambitious Lieutenant Colonel Thomas Gage of the Forty-fourth Foot. He proposed to raise a weak battalion of five companies on his own and to be reimbursed if the Crown approved. Both Loudoun and the king gave their approval, and Gage gained his colonelcy in the summer of 1758.[39]

Loudoun and his commanders were beginning to realize the limitations of provincial rangers. Experience revealed that only Rogers could control them—but not all the time. Like Indians, they were excessively fond of rum and went out on patrol only when it pleased them. They also had a tendency to riot when exposed to regular discipline. Yet they were expanded to nine companies, including one of Christian Mahican Indians from Stockbridge, Massachusetts, for the campaign of 1758.

Perhaps most significant was the adaptation of the regular battalions. In 1756, at the urging of several Swiss soldiers of fortune in the British service, the Crown decided to raise in Pennsylvania and New York a sort of foreign legion for American service. It was a regiment of German-speaking Americans of four battalions, with many foreign officers. They were trained "to fire at Marks, and in order to qualify them for the service of the Woods, they are to be taught to load and fire, lyeing on the Ground and kneeling. They are to be taught to march in Order, slow and fast in all sortes of Ground.

---

[38]John C. Fuller, *British Light Infantry in the Eighteenth Century* (London: Hutchinson, 1925), is vague, very brief, and unreliable, but it is the only book on the subject. For a stimulating essay on the doctrinal legacy of light infantry development, see Peter Paret, "Colonial Experience and European Military Reform at the End of the Eighteenth Century," *Journal of the Institute for Army Historical Research* 37 (1959): 47–59. The best account of the role of British light infantry in America is in Eric Robson, "British Light Infantry in the Eighteenth Century: The Effect of American Conditions," *Army and Defense Quarterly* 62 (1952): 209–22.

[39]Pargellis, *Lord Loudoun,* pp. 304–05; WO 34 (Amherst Papers), bundle 46a, has Gage's proposal to Loudoun of November 1757, and Gage's orders to raise the unit are in bundle 72; Forbes, *Writings,* pp. 216–17. The Eightieth Foot had brown jackets rather than red.

They are frequently to pitch & fold up their Tents, and to be accustomed to pack up and carry their necessaries in the most commodious manner."[40]

But the new regiment, the Sixtieth Foot or Royal Americans, was not a light infantry unit.[41] It was dressed like the regulars but without lace on its uniform. All the regiments in America were being trained to skirmish by this time and, if an ambush erupted, soldiers followed the orders to "tree all."[42] British officers began to recognize the value of patrolling both to keep enemy Indians at a distance and to acclimate their men.[43] In the summer of 1758 one officer wrote: "You would laugh to see the droll figure we cut. Regular and Provincials are ordered to cut the brims of their hats off. The Regulars as well as the Provincials have left off their proper regimentals, that is, they have cut their coats so as to scarcely reach their waist. You would not distinguish us from common plough men."[44] In addition, other efforts were made to adapt the troops to

[40]Loudoun Papers, 2421, cited in Pargellis, *Lord Loudoun*, pp. 299–300.

[41]Lewis Butler, *The Annals of the King's Royal Rifle Corps*, vol. 1, "The Royal Americans" (London: Smith, Elder, 1913), makes the mistake of calling the Royal Americans light infantry. He confuses the earlier unit with the Sixtieth Foot when it was a crack light infantry unit in the Napoleonic era. The four battalions of the Sixtieth never were considered light infantry, were not trained as such, and were never used as such. In addition, they later had light infantry companies as did other line battalions. While it is true that James Prevost, commander of the Fourth Battalion/Sixtieth Foot, urged in May 1757 that American units be raised and trained in light infantry style, including the use of whistles and Indian-chasing dogs, there is no evidence that the plan was ever accepted or that Prevost made such innovations in his own battalion. Prevost to Cumberland, "Mémoire sur la Guerre d'Amérique," in Pargellis, *Military Affairs*, pp. 337–40.

[42]Pargellis, *Lord Loudoun*, p. 300.

[43]Memorandum of General John Forbes, written at New York, December 18, 1757, in Forbes, *Writings*, p. 24. A few months later, when leading his army across the wilderness to the Forks of the Ohio, Forbes wrote to Lieutenant Colonel Bouquet of the First Battalion/Sixtieth Foot (in ibid., p. 125): "I must confess in this country, wee must comply and learn the Art of Warr, from Ennemy Indians or anything else who have seen the country and Warr carried on in it."

[44]Letter of anonymous officer at Flatbush, Long Island, June 13, 1758, in Cecil P. Lawson, *A History of the Uniforms of the British Army*, 5 vols. (London: Peter Davies et al., 1940–67), 4:77–78.

their environment. The troops carried in their haversacks thirty pounds of meal, which they cooked for themselves. Knapsacks often were discarded, and the soldiers wore blanket rolls like the rangers. In June 1758, ten rifles were issued to each battalion to arm the best marksmen.[45]

The model for regimental adaptation was the Fifty-fifth Foot, and the model of personnel adaptation was its colonel, George Augustus, Viscount Howe. Howe made his regiment over in the image of the rangers; its uniform, however, remained the traditional red. An observant young woman remembered that

> Lord Howe always lay . . . with the regiment which he commanded and which he modelled in such a manner that they were ever after considered an example to the whole American army. . . . Above the pedantry of holding up standards of military rules where it was impossible to practice them, and the narrow spirit of preferring the modes of his own country . . . Lord Howe laid aside all pride and prejudice, and gratefully accepted counsel from those whom he knew to be best qualified to direct them.[46]

As a result of these changes one soldier could write in 1758 that "The art of War is much changed and improved here. I suppose by the end of the summer it will have undergone a total Revolution. . . . Our hair is about an inch long; . . . hats . . . are worn slouched. . . . Coats are docked. . . . The Highlanders have put on breeches. . . . Swords and sashes are degraded, and many have taken up the Hatchet and wear Tomahawks."[47] Thus the army that Loudoun left owed much to his flexibility and attention to detail, even if Abercromby thought military affairs were more backward at

[45]Norreys Jephson O'Conor, *A Servant of the Crown in England and North America, 1756–1761* . . . (New York: D. Appleton-Century, 1938), p. 96.

[46]Ann Grant, *Memoirs of an American Lady* . . . , 2 vols. (London: Longman, Hurst, Rees, and Orme, 1809), 1:199–200.

[47]Dr. Richard Huck-Saunders to Jan Ingenhousz, May 18, 1758, microfilm copy in the Ingenhousz letters, American Philosophical Society, Philadelphia.

Loudoun's departure than when he first appeared.[48] Amherst, as commander in chief, was indebted to his predecessors for his improved army of 1759. The major challenge that he faced was to use this army, now adapted to American conditions, to best advantage.

Amherst took measures that winter to check the activities of French and Indians near his cantonments.[49] He ordered that a pursuit force of rangers always be ready at Fort Edward. He wrote of the Indian raiders: "Once overtaken they are very easily beat, and they won't like returning again . . ."[50] Gage was less sanguine than Amherst, as he wrote to Lieutenant Colonel Frederick Haldimand in February: "I don't imagine we shall ever overtake them by a pursuit in the Woods. The only chance to come up with them in my opinion is not to pursue but to send a Party to take a sweep around and try and hit them."[51] Gage also wrote to Amherst at the same time that Haldimand

> will use all means to Chastise them when they next make their appearance: But I despair of this being done by Rangers, judging from the many pursuits of those people after the Indians during my service in this Country, in which they have never once come up with them. The Light Infantry of the Regiment headed by a briske Officer with some of the boldest Rangers mixed with Them, to prevent their being lost in the Woods, will be the most likely people to Effect this service.[52]

[48]Abercromby to General Lawrence, Governor of Nova Scotia, April 30, 1758, Abercromby Papers, Henry E. Huntington Library, San Marino, California.

[49]Amherst to Gage, February 10, 1759, Amherst Letters, vol. 4, William L. Clements Library, Ann Arbor, Michigan.

[50]Ibid.

[51]Gage to Haldimand, February 20, 1759, Gage Letter Book, Clements Library. Gage assured Major Clephane, who was in charge of Fort Stanwix, that men who captured or killed Indian raiders would be well rewarded. "Prisoners are troublesome. I look upon these partys as so many assassins, not soldiers, therefore they have no quarter." Gage to Clephane, March 16, 1759, Gage Letter Book.

[52]Gage to Amherst, February 18, 1759, ibid.

When led by Rogers, the rangers could be very effective. On March 3, 1759, Rogers led a picked force of 358 men, consisting of 52 Iroquois Indians, 169 light infantry of the Royal Americans, 47 men of the Royal Regiment (Second Battalion/First Regiment of Foot), and 90 rangers, to scout Fort Carillon at Ticonderoga. Lieutenant Diedrich Brehm, an engineer attached to the First Battalion of the Sixtieth Foot, accompanied the party. Brehm spent most of one moonlit night flat on his stomach in the snow on a mountain overlooking Fort Carillon. He sketched the fort and later crept up to a new French log barrier replacing the one Montcalm had built to thwart Abercromby. There Brehm examined the fort at close hand. The ensuing raid was a big success: only a few men were lost, though others were severely frostbitten.[53] The party returned with five scalps, five prisoners, and valuable information about the fort, despite having been twice pursued by the enemy. The conduct of the British Indians with Rogers was less than admirable. Half of the original force of Indians had disappeared on the course of their well-lubricated journey from the Mohawk Valley to Fort Edward. On the return trip, the Indians shot a Highland sentry in the leg.

Although Rogers was anxious to use one or two companies of Stockbridge Indians in the campaign of 1759, Gage was less impressed with their abilities. He informed Amherst that "These Indians were last Campaign a great Nuisance to the Army, and did no manner of service; some People say they were not properly managed, I own myself ignorant of the management that is proper for those Gentry; can only say that neither orders or Entreatys could prevail on them to do service, always lying drunk in their Hutts, or firing round the camp."[54] Amherst nevertheless gave permission for two companies of Stockbridge warriors to be raised for the rangers,

---

[53]Rogers's journal of this expedition, his examination of the prisoners, and Brehm's description of Carillon are in WO 34, vol. 46A.

[54]Gage to Amherst, February 24, 1759, ibid.

though he had his doubts about using any Indians. He wrote Gage that

> I know what a vile brew they are and I have as bad an opinion of lazy rum drinking scoundrels as any one can have, I shall however take them into His Majesty's Service for this next campaign, to keep them from doing mischief elsewhere, and as I am in hopes we shall be able to act offensively and successfully, they may be of more service than what they have hitherto been. The French are afraid of them, and though they have but very little reason for it, it will be right not only to keep up their terror but to increase it as much as we can, which the name of numbers will do, and I shall for that reason engage as many of them as I can for the ensuing campaign.[55]

Major Rogers began early in 1759 to recruit his rangers to full strength for the opening of the campaign. Amherst put advertisements in newspapers and wrote colonial officials calling for volunteers for the rangers. Recruits began slowly to join Rogers in March; by the beginning of May he had reassembled most of his corps. Joseph Gorham's rangers, the best and least expensive of the ranger organizations, according to Amherst, had remained in service in Nova Scotia over the winter.[56] Despite his use of over 1,000 rangers in New York alone in 1759, Amherst did not discard the concept of regular light infantrymen.

During the winter the regulars were taught a new type of drill that had been imported from the army of Frederick the Great.[57] Although this development may appear to imply that the army was

[55]Amherst to Gage, February 20, 1759, Amherst Letters, vol. 4, Clements Library. Amherst also wrote to Gage a month later: "Capt. Jacobs has behaved just like himself and all the drunken good for nothing tribe, I hate them all, but as things are they may do some good by doing mischief of which we have a great deal to do [to] be at par with the French." Amherst to Gage, March 26, 1759, Amherst Letters, vol. 4, Clements Library.

[56]Amherst to Charles Lawrence, March 9, 1759, WO 34, vol. 46A.

[57]Amherst, "General Orders," December 13, 1758, Amherst Papers, Public Archives of Canada, P58. Translations of the Prussian infantry regulations were published in London in 1754 and 1757. The best book on the training of the British army in this period is J. A. Houlding, *Fit for Service: The Training of the British Army, 1715–1795* (New York: Oxford University Press, 1981).

becoming more European and more formalistic in its training, it was really a sign of flexibility of outlook. The footsore musketeers of the Prussian king had for three years fought off far greater numbers of their enemies, partly by having better generals, partly by having better tactics and training. No wonder that their allies should try to emulate them. At the same time, the British generals in North America had seen the need for "light-armed foot" as a result of their own experiences in the New World. Amherst strongly approved of the idea of light infantry. In February 1759 he ordered one-tenth of each regular battalion formed into a light infantry corps.[58] An officer on Amherst's staff wrote of the decision: "We have chosen out one hundred men from each regiment, and pitched upon the officers to act this year as light infantry; they are clothed and accoutered as light as possible and in my opinion are a kind of troops that has been much wanted in this country. They have what ammunition they want, so that I don't doubt but they will be excellent marksmen."[59]

To facilitate the movement of light infantrymen through the brush, Amherst ordered in May that they be equipped with carbines in place of muskets.[60] Like the rangers, the light infantry were trained to "swing pack" at a moment's notice and move swiftly through the wilderness; in addition, they possessed the discipline and staying power of regulars. Amherst was also pleased to note that American volunteers had quickly filled up the depleted ranks of Gage's light infantry. He remarked that "the Yankees love dearly a brown coat."[61] In terms of light infantry, the army was well prepared for the campaign of 1759.

Pitt's great plan for the campaign of 1759 was ambitious in scope and objective. He ordered Amherst to advance into the heart of Canada after capturing the stronghold of Fort Carillon; Wolfe was to

[58]Gage to Amherst, February 24, 1759, WO 34, vol. 46A.

[59]Captain Roger Townshend to Major Robert Rogers, February 26, 1759, in Rogers, *Journals*, ed. Hough, pp. 97–98.

[60]Amherst to James Furnis, comptroller of ordnance in North America, May 5, 1759, WO 34, vol. 79.

[61]Amherst to Ligonier, January 18, 1759, Amherst Slipcase, Clements Library, and Public Archives of Canada, P11.

seize Quebec; other commands would assist. Pitt desired nothing less than the conquest of Canada in 1759. Spring was a time of preparation—no offensive could be launched until the provincials had assembled after spring planting. The regulars drilled, the rangers scouted, supplies and equipment were readied and moved forward. At the beginning of May, Amherst began to mass his army of 5,500 regulars and 5,000 provincials above Albany.[62] The last of the colonial contingents would arrive six weeks later, much to the annoyance of the impatient Amherst.

At about this time Amherst introduced for the first time in the British army the celebrated two-deep "thin red line" formation that would often be seen in the American Revolution, and would win undying fame in the Peninsular War, at Waterloo, and at Balaclava. By standing order, Amherst told his troops to reduce their firing lines from three ranks to two because "the enemy have very few regular troops to oppose us, and no yelling of Indians, or fire of Canadians, can possibly withstand two ranks, if the men are silent, attentive, and obedient to their officers."[63]

Major Robert Rogers's corps of rangers was ready to take the field with a fresh strength of 800 men. Unhappily, many rangers were new to irregular warfare. Amherst complained to Gage, his able assistant: "they are the most unknowing for every part of the Service that is to be conceived, at their rate of going on they must always be beat, I have tried to rub them up and show them the way to march in woods for those I have had with me know nothing of the matter."[64] Nevertheless, Rogers supplied valuable information about the French at Carillon. His rangers were constantly skirmishing with the French Indians and bushlopers after warm weather returned.

Amherst was much more concerned, of course, with the forwarding of supplies and troops to the camps and posts above

[62]Gage Papers, American Series, vol. 2, Clements Library.
[63]Knox, *Historical Journal*, 1:487–88.
[64]Amherst to Gage, June 6, 1759, Amherst Letters, vol. 4, Clements Library.

Albany—most of which was the task of Bradstreet's bateaux corps. Bradstreet had had great difficulty finding volunteers for his transport service. Lured by the high bounties of provincial regiments and repelled by the hard labor of the transport network, colonial volunteers were scarce in 1759.[65] The upshot was that there were only enough bateauxmen to provide transport for an expedition against Niagara led by General John Prideaux. Amherst was obliged to resort to an expedient of 1758: having combat troops, particularly provincials, carry forward their own provisions in stages. This scheme had not been very successful the previous year. The troops were overworked, many provisions had spoiled, and many draft animals had been ruined. Since the provincials despised such grueling labor, desertions increased.

As the tempo of the campaign quickened, problems increased. Heavy rains in May turned the roads to seas of mud and swept from the shoreline of the Mohawk River a number of bateaux and whaleboats inexpertly stored by provincials in 1758. Quick action by Amherst saved most of the river craft from plunging over Cohoes Falls. Amherst gave orders reminding the army of the need for constant vigilance: "all detachments will keep out Flanking Partys whether they come in Batteaus or march as the commanding officer will judge necessary, that it may not be in the power of any Skulking Party of the Enemy to surprise and scalp any that are careless."[66] As ever, the troops were drilled in alternate firing and in marksmanship.

Amherst's army, well supplied and well trained, moved down Lake George in late June and easily took Forts Carillon and St. Frédéric. Prideaux and his successor, Gage, captured Niagara. In each offensive, the supply system worked well. The French did have a surprise for Amherst on Lake Champlain: a fleet of four vessels. That tiny flotilla was enough to smash an unprotected British armada of bateaux and whaleboats. Amherst had no recourse but to

---

[65]Bradstreet to Horatio Gates, August 21, 1759, Gage Papers, American Series, vol. 3, Clements Library.

[66]Amherst to Captain Robert Prescott, June 14, 1759, WO 34, vol. 80.

build warships of his own to gain control of Champlain. He worried constantly about Wolfe's progress before Quebec, but he could neither send aid nor put more pressure on the French. Gage, having taken Niagara, disobeyed Amherst's orders to move on to Montreal. While Amherst built ships he also rebuilt Fort Carillon and renamed it Fort Ticonderoga. He built a strong new fort at Crown Point as well. These posts would be key supply depots in the eventual conquest of Canada.

Only by mid-September were the British vessels ready. They easily outmaneuvered and took the French craft. Two obstacles remained: the French fort at Isle-au-Noix and the storms of early autumn. Amherst learned at this time that Wolfe had captured Quebec, but most of its defenders had escaped to Montreal and possibly to Isle-au-Noix. With total victory in sight, Amherst reluctantly postponed the conquest of Canada until 1760.[67] While his army was halted at Lake Champlain, Amherst decided to remove one troublesome military factor in this and future campaigns. Angered at the constant pinprick attacks of the Abenaki Indians, the most numerous Indian allies of the French, he decided to destroy their main village of St. François (St. Francis), near the St. Lawrence. He told Robert Rogers to take 200 rangers and "Remember the Barbarities that have been committed by the enemy's Indian scoundrels. Take your revenge, but don't forget that, though those dastardly villains have promiscuously murdered women and children of all ages, it is my order that no women or children be killed or hurt."[68] The rangers were delighted "to chastise these savages with some severity."[69] For years the St. Francis Indians had terrorized the

---

[67]For details see Daniel J. Beattie, "General Jeffery Amherst and the Conquest of Canada, 1758–1760" (Ph.D. diss., Duke University, 1975; published version, Ann Arbor: University Microfilms, 1976); and Jeffery Amherst, *The Journal of Jeffery Amherst . . .* , ed. John C. Webster (Toronto: Ryerson, 1931).

[68]Robert Rogers, *The Journals of Robert Rogers*, ed. Howard H. Peckham (New York: Corinth, 1961), p. 144.

[69]Ibid.

New England frontier; many rangers had lost kin and friends to the Abenakis.

Crossing 200 miles of wild terrain to get to St. Francis was difficult even for the rangers. One-quarter of their strength melted away because of sickness, lameness, and injuries, even before reaching St. Francis. But they did surprise the Indian town, kill between 100 and 200 inhabitants, and burn the place down. Rogers lost only two men in the massacre; he lost many more on the way home by not exercising more discipline over his raiders. Before stumbling into the Connecticut Valley settlements, one-third of his hungry men fell prey to enraged pursuers and to starvation. Yet the raid was a great success. It dealt a sharp blow to the morale of the French and their red allies. There were no sanctuaries now: Amherst's raiders could penetrate deep into Canada.

Amherst formed another anti-Indian expedition in early 1760 to punish the Cherokees who were attacking the frontiers of the Carolinas and Virginia. He sent south a crack force of 1,300 regulars, including 400 Highlanders. The Highlanders may have welcomed the sight of the mountains in Cherokee country. Their commander, Colonel Archibald Montgomery, was undoubtedly glad to have such sturdy mountaineers in his force. The expedition punished the Cherokees but discovered that it had only enough pack horses to carry either provisions or the British wounded. In these circumstances Montgomery decided to rejoin Amherst. The skill-fully led expedition was thus a failure, and its retreat actually encouraged the Indians. Another expedition the following year would settle the matter.

The skill of the British army in crossing the wilderness was never more obvious than in 1760. Amherst ordered a three-pronged advance on what was left of French power at Montreal. One army, under Amherst himself, advanced up the Mohawk, across Lake Ontario, and down the St. Lawrence to Montreal. Another pincer advanced on Montreal from Quebec. A third took Isle-au-Noix and approached Montreal from the south. All three armies gathered outside the crumbling walls of the city within a forty-eight-hour period.[70] New France surrendered on September 8, 1760.

The last campaign of the war went so smoothly, with few casualties and little delay, that it is easy to underestimate it. Seventeen thousand regulars and provincials crossed hundreds of miles of wilderness to meet at Montreal. It was a British logistical triumph. The rangers, Iroquois, and light regulars who came to Montreal show that it was also a victory for the use of auxiliaries in American campaigns. Both bateauxmen and light troops eased the passage of the regulars and provincials.

There would be other campaigns ahead even though New France had fallen. The French still held Martinique and other valuable sugar islands, and the Spanish would be attacked at Havana. The Cherokee were to be chastised. In 1763, the colonial frontier would be set alight again by Pontiac's uprising. In these campaigns and in later ones in America and Europe, the British army would profit from its adaptation to wilderness conditions.

The British army met problems in the French and Indian War unlike any in the Old World. New and extraordinary logistical and tactical problems had to be solved to enable the army to cross rugged terrain and great distances. The men in the ranks, already accustomed to grueling labor, rigid discipline, and the ravages of camp diseases, had to overcome their fears of Indians and the oppressive presence of the American forest. The army that entered Montreal in triumph in 1760, took Havana in 1762, held out at Detroit and Fort Pitt, and won at Bushy Run was still basically a European army, using European weapons, tactics, organization, and administration. Like the redcoats at Minden, the troops in America wore red and carried flintlock muskets. Unlike their comrades in Europe, they took aim at their opponents. Battalions formed up in ranks at Quebec and Ticonderoga and Louisbourg in formations not very different from those at Dettingen and Fontenoy. Fighting alongside the British in America, however, were troops that made warfare

---

[70]Amherst, *Journal*, p. 247.

there different: rangers, Indians, combat boatmen, and regular light infantry. Those auxiliary troops, irregulars, smoothed the way across the wilderness for the regulars and permitted them to fight decisive battles in the European manner—the only way technology and training allowed.

Intelligence and logistics, the probing feelers and extenuated tail of an army, were developed to let the forces of George II and George III crawl through the forest to victory. A way had been found to make war in such a country.

A World Uncertain
and Strongly Checker'd

SHEILA L. SKEMP

*I*t took a cast-iron stomach, a lot of capital, and a good dose of luck to survive the vicissitudes of trade that characterized the merchant's life in mid-eighteenth-century Newport, Rhode Island, during the War of Austrian Succession and the Seven Years' War. Indeed the city's bright hopes for a future of unending prosperity were almost gone by 1765. This did not mean that everybody failed or that the picture was one of unending and unmitigated disaster. It did mean, however, that Newport's fortunes were, as merchant Roland Cotton described them, "uncertain and strongly Checker'd."[1] And it was the insecurity and instability, the not knowing from one year to the next, or even one day to the next, what was going to happen to them that so troubled the city's inhabitants.

The problem, as the merchants saw it, came from England. Their failures were not the result of poor business practices, inattention to detail, or sheer loss of nerve. They were doing the same things they had always done, using techniques that, on balance at least, had served them very well in the past. But now nothing seemed to work.

[1]Roland Cotton to Samuel Vernon, May 30, 1743, Lopez and Vernon Papers, Box 48, folder 3, p. 400, Newport Historical Society, Newport, Rhode Island (hereafter cited as NHS).

And nothing worked because the merchants of Newport, after twenty years of almost uninterrupted peace, found themselves once again drawn into Britain's imperial struggles with France and Spain. They were forced to carry on their social, political, and economic lives on terms dictated by the exigencies of war, war they had neither declared nor even wanted. These terms were not necessarily disadvantageous. Many entrepreneurs survived and even prospered during the War of Austrian Succession (1740–48), while others even managed to come out of the more damaging Seven Years' War (1756–63) relatively unscathed.[2] Most of them faced and survived the wars of the mid-eighteenth century as they continued to exploit old and proven methods of trade, while a few brave souls even experimented with totally new commercial relationships. At the end of both wars, however, Rhode Island was assailed by economic depression, causing many merchants to begin investing an increasingly large share of their capital in safer noncommercial activity. And a few abandoned the rigors of trade altogether.

Nor was it just the merchants whose lives were altered as a result of British foreign policy. The fate of the lower and middling sort in the town was also inextricably linked to the fortunes of war. While continuity with the past, not qualitative changes in life-style or expectations for the future, characterized their existence throughout much of the period, those changes that did occur can be traced to the social and economic dislocations brought about by the wars. The world of artisans and shopkeepers, sailors and workers was also "uncertain and strongly Checker'd."

The effect of war on Newport's economy was mixed. For some it was even a blessing. The requirements of war not only supplied

[2]Colonial merchants were generally optimistic about possibilities presented by the war. They were particularly hopeful that their forays in Canada, especially the Louisbourg expedition, might result in a free port there, thus opening new avenues for lucrative trade. Admiral Sir Peter Warren to Governor Joseph Wanton, November 26, 1745, in John R. Bartlett, *Records of the Colony of Rhode Island and Providence Plantations in New England, 1664–1798* (hereafter cited as *RICR*), 10 vols. (Providence: Knowles Anthony, 1858), 5:149.

employment for workers but also offered consumers for goods provided by the city's artisans and victuallers. Merchants like Jonathan Nichols, Christopher Champlin, John Cranston, and Joseph Whipple used their influence to obtain government contracts to supply both colonial troops and members of the king's navy with rum, food, and provisions. Investors in Newport's shipbuilding industry profited from the increased government purchase of colony sloops fitted out to protect the city's harbor from enemy attack. Only in 1757 was Newport's monopoly of government shipbuilding contracts even threatened.[3]

War was not, of course, an unmixed blessing to Newport's economy. Because of its exposed position, the city had more expenses than any other Rhode Island town. Consequently it had to build a guardhouse, appoint a military watch, and donate some funds toward the financing of Fort George, which was erected and maintained primarily for the city's protection. An artillery company, headed by many of Newport's leading merchants, was also created to meet wartime exigencies. The colony was reluctant to tax its inhabitants in order to secure the necessary funds for these projects; thus it relied on lotteries and loans from the merchants, who in many cases were already caught in an unreliable and sometimes disastrous commercial situation as a result of war. The colony's creditors assumed that their loans would be repaid with interest, for the British government had repeatedly promised that they would be reimbursed in full for their wartime expenditures. But the immediate effect of the loans was nevertheless often felt by those merchants who contributed heavily to the colony's efforts

[3]MS. 11, Freebody Papers, Rhode Island Historical Society, Providence (hereafter cited as RIHS), p. 83; *RICR*, 5:6, 16, 90–92, 101, 121, 123, 128–29, 422; Christopher Champlin to Christopher Champlin, Jr., August 24, 1764, in *Commerce of Rhode Island 1726–1800*, 2 vols. (Massachusetts Historical Society, *Collections*, 9 and 10, ser. 7), 1:11–12; John Banister to Benjamin Jones, June 29, 1748, John Banister Letterbook, 1748–50, NHS, p. 31; *Acts and Laws of His Majesty's Colony of Rhode Island and Providence Plantations in America* (Newport: James and Anne Franklin, 1744), pp. 235, 236.

throughout both wars.[4] They advanced nearly £8,000 for a twenty-gun ship used in the Louisbourg expedition, paid officers and soldiers for that same expedition, and helped as well to finance the abortive attack on Annapolis at a time when none of their previous expenditures had been reimbursed.[5]

War disrupted Newport's economy in less obvious ways as well. It created occasional dislocations in the city, as French prisoners who were taken by privateers or the colony militia were housed in the jail at town expense. Moreover, Newport was occasionally forced to cope with large numbers of soldiers who inundated the town after expeditions against the French. After the colony's participation in the "loyal tho' unsuccessful undertaking" against Annapolis in 1746, for instance, Newport was flooded with returning soldiers, many of whom were sick or impoverished. All of these men had to be cared for and fed at town expense.[6]

War also made it more difficult for the city's overworked officials to maintain order. Deserters from other colonies often engaged in drunken revelries and petty crime. Soldiers "wasted, embezzled and damnified" their weapons and supplies. Many turned profiteer and sold for a tidy sum weapons provided by the colony. Occasional riots against the king's officers who arrived in Newport to apprehend deserters or recruit soldiers had to be contained. All of this activity,

---

[4]Newport, Town Meeting Records, NHS, p. 141; *RICR*, 5:35–36, 39–40, 290; 6:18. When Newport, drained by the expenses of war, announced its inability to meet its obligations to the poor, the merchants came to the rescue and loaned sufficient funds to the town treasury. Newport, Town Meeting Recs., p. 189.

[5]*RICR*, 5:194. Godfrey Malbone went so far as to try to raise 500 men for the Louisbourg expedition singlehandedly, and he personally led his troops to Massachusetts where preparations for the expedition were taking place. Ibid., pp. 105, 505, 146, 154; Governor Wanton to Governor Shirley and Admiral Charles Knowles, October 23, 1747, ibid., pp. 230–31.

[6]*RICR*, 5:122; *Petitions of the Rhode Island General Assembly, 1725–1860*, 72 vols., Rhode Island Archives, Providence, 4:103; *Reports, 1728–1860*, 14 vols., RI Archives, 1:16.

in what had previously been a town of under 7,000 people, caused consternation and expense to the inhabitants of Newport.[7]

But it was the effect of war on the economy that was ultimately felt most strongly by the people of Newport. And in a town dominated by commercial capital, that effect was felt first by the merchants. There were, of course, wartime opportunities that tantalized some entrepreneurs. Nothing so stirred their romantic inclinations, their love of adventure, and their desire for wealth as the chance of privateering. Recalling the success privateers had enjoyed in the War of Spanish Succession (1701–13), many were only too eager to invest in such ventures again. The colonial government encouraged privateers at the outbreak of war in 1739 and again in 1755. Indeed, the governors often excused Newport's inability to raise sufficient troops for the war effort because of the "scarcity of men" due to a "spirit of privateering which much prevails since the Spanish war."[8] Figures indicate that the governors' point was well taken. Five privateers had already been equipped by January 1740; by the fall of 1744, fourteen were out and two more were preparing to leave momentarily; and at least fifty privateers had been fitted out between 1755 and 1760, according to Governor Hopkins.[9]

[7]*RICR*, 5:107; 6:52, 154, 186–87; Andrew Stone to the Governor of Rhode Island, October 1, 1743, in Gertrude S. Kimball, *Correspondence of the Colonial Governors of Rhode Island, 1723–1775*, 2 vols. (Boston: Houghton Mifflin, 1902), p. 325; Evarts B. Green and Virginia D. Harrington, *American Population Before the Federal Census of 1780* (Gloucester: Peter Smith, 1916), p. 67.

[8]Samuel Ward to General Amherst, May 27, 1762, in *Letters from the Governors*, 4 vols., RI Archives, 1:125; Samuel Ward to Earl of Egremont, August 6, 1762, *RICR*, 6:344. Ward was probably not exaggerating the problem. In 1758, for instance, Rhode Island claimed that over 1,500 able-bodied men were out in privateers. None of these men was willing to serve the king when profits could be made elsewhere. *Reports*, 2:65.

[9]William P. Sheffield, "Privateers and Privateersmen of Newport," *Newport Mercury*, April 10 and June 5, 1880; Rhode Island Public Notary Records, 1648–1776, 8 vols., RI Archives, vols. 5–7; Alexander Hamilton, *Gentleman's Progress: The Itinerarium of Dr. Alexander Hamilton, 1744*, ed. Carl Bridenbaugh (Chapel Hill: University of North Carolina Press, 1948), p. 56; *Boston News-Letter*, August 23, 1739; *Boston*

But the world of the privateer also was "uncertain and strongly Checker'd." Many merchants profited from their activity, while others were nearly destroyed by it, and virtually no one came away without suffering a disastrous loss or two. Privateering always entailed great risks, and losers considerably outnumbered winners in that precarious business. Consider the fate of one of Newport's wealthiest and most powerful merchants, Godfrey Malbone. At the beginning of the War of Austrian Succession, he immediately began fitting out privateers, and at first his investments resulted in enormous profits. After the French entered the war in 1744, however, he suffered prolonged reversals, and by 1746 he was experiencing difficulty in scraping together enough money to fit out more ships. It never occurred to Malbone to abandon his efforts, and he stubbornly refused to "give over." Only a man of his wealth and connections could have sustained such losses, and even he was forced to bring his son home from Oxford because he was unable to support him there.[10]

The problems facing privateers were numerous. Adventurers could never be sure that they would find and capture a valuable prize. Captain Michael Ryan of the *Harlequin* sailed into Newport harbor in the fall of 1762 after an unsuccessful cruise of four months during which he had met only one potential prize, and his attempt to capture it had ended in disaster. He lost eight men and "had the additional mortification of not bringing off the prizes." Privateers were constantly faced with stiff competition, which increased steadily so long as the war endured. Vessels were often forced to share

---

Evening-Post, April 2, 1740; *Boston Post Boy*, June 9, 1740; Samuel Ward to Board of Trade, January 9, 1740, *RICR*, 5:12; Governor Hopkins to Secretary Pitt, December 20, 1760, *RICR*, 6:264; *Boston Gazette*, September 11, 1744.

[10]Mrs. Godfrey Malbone to Godfrey Malbone, Jr., October 6, 1746; Godfrey Malbone to Godfrey Malbone, Jr., October 7, 1746; Edward Scott to Godfrey Malbone, Jr., August 4, 1746, Malbone Papers, RIHS.

their paltry prizes with other ships that invariably appeared on the horizon just in time for the kill.[11]

Once a prize was brought into port, an owner's worries were by no means ended. Captured cargoes were often the subject of prolonged litigation as their original owners used every maneuver available to prove that their vessels had been taken illegally. Sometimes their claims were justified, for privateer crews often failed to distinguish between enemy and neutral ships. But other times the accusations were frivolous and unfair. Metcalf Bowler, in particular, was often involved in litigation over the disposal of his prizes, costing him dearly in time and money. It is doubtful that many merchants escaped without at least one lengthy bout with the Admiralty Courts.[12]

Privateering was a potentially profitable and entirely legal activity, but Newport merchants engaged in other affairs that put them well beyond the bounds of law. Their trade with French and Spanish enemies was particularly offensive to British authorities. Even when it was conducted within legal strictures, few could deny that it violated the spirit of the law. Yet trade with the enemy

---

[11]*Newport Mercury*, December 26, 1758, October 5, and September 13, 1762; Howard M. Chapin, Privateer Notes, 1755–62, RIHS; *Phenix vs. Magdalene*, 1744, in Dorothy S. Towle, ed., *Records of the Vice-Admiralty Court of Rhode Island, 1716–1752* (Washington, D.C.: American Historical Association, 1936), pp. 284–85; also *Prince Frederick vs. Postillion*, 1746, and *Charming Betty and Reprisal vs. Endragh*, 1747/48, ibid., pp. 397–98, 440–41; In the Matter of the Capture of the Ship *South Kingston* and her Cargo, Chapin, Privateer Cases, RIHS; Joseph Crawford, Log Book Kept by Capt. Joseph Crawford on the Sloop *Roby*, August 17 to November 2, 1759, RIHS.

[12]A. J. Forsch to Governor of Rhode Island, July 30, 1743, in *Letters to the Governors, 1731–1849*, 24 vols., RI Archives, 2:34; John Livingston to Metcalf Bowler and Co., July 28, 1738, Champlin Papers, box 4, folder E, RIHS; In the Matter of the Prize Ship the *San Francisco*, alias *Peregrin*; Lords Commissioners of Prizes, *The William Galley*, Chapin, Privateer Cases; James Allen vs. Ship *Angola*, 1743; John Griffith vs. Snow *Caulker*, 1743; *Reprisal* and *Trelaner vs. Young Benjamin*, 1747; *St. Andrew* vs. *Nooyt Godegt*, 1742; John Dennis vs. Joseph Wanton, 1746; Petition of John Seet, 1747—all in Towle, *Vice-Admiralty Court*, pp. 198–223, 442–43, 184–88, 342–43, 409–10.

continued throughout the mid-eighteenth century, as entrepreneurs continued to search for the cheapest products and the best markets.[13] Merchants did not view this trade as unpatriotic, and they certainly did not see themselves as traitors to the Crown. For most Newport merchants, war was simply a time when greater precautions had to be taken in following a profitable and necessary trading pattern. In war as in peace, the most profitable action continued to be the most desirable.

Illegal trade with the enemy took many forms. Sometimes Newport merchants traded with the French through neutral ports. In the War of Austrian Succession, their favorite ports were Surinam and St. Eustatius; during the Seven Years' War, Monte Cristi on the Spanish half of the island of Hispaniola was the primary target. There is also some indication that Rhode Island merchants traded with the French in Florida, Louisiana, and especially South Carolina. Other trade was carried on under the auspices of transient French merchants who resided temporarily in Newport and brought goods from Cape Breton and Cape François. Still other merchants used flags of truce, ostensibly as a means of exchanging prisoners of war with the enemy, but in fact as a means of gaining access to French markets.[14]

---

[13]George Louis Beer has no doubt that trade with the enemy in this period was unequivocally illegal. *British Colonial Policy, 1754–1765* (New York: Peter Smith, 1933), p. 72. There is, however, some room for doubt. Merchants often asserted that trade with the enemy was acceptable if it did not involve supplies or provisions that would enable the other side to carry on the war more effectively. Trade with the French and Spanish through neutral ports was also a ticklish question, for if the colonists traded at legal ports, using middlemen as conduits for their goods, it was doubtful that they could be held responsible for the subsequent disposition of those goods.

[14]Joseph Sherwood to Governor Hopkins, May 30, 1761, in Kimball, *Correspondence*, 2:320; General Amherst to the Governor of Rhode Island, May 7, 1762, and General Amherst to Governor Hopkins, April 15, 1762, *RICR*, 6:318, 312; Richard Chillcolt to Godfrey Malbone, Jr., March 17, 1750, Malbone Papers; *Notary Records*, 7:243; James Birket, *Some Cursory Remarks Made by James Birket in His Voyage to North America, 1730–1751* (New Haven: Yale University Press, 1916), p. 30; *Rhode Island Equity*

It is impossible to state exactly how many merchants engaged in illegal trade. For obvious reasons, Newport's entrepreneurs were reluctant to leave evidence of their involvement. Many were like Captain Fones Hazard, who took a "pretended" voyage to Antigua but somehow ended up on the island of Hispaniola instead.[15] Others were like Captain James Duncan, who signed his letters "you know whome" whenever he was engaged in questionable activities. And there were merchants like Christopher Champlin and John Banister who traded regularly with the French through neutral ports but who carefully gave their captains very general and unincriminating instructions. Banister was particularly circumspect, often specifically warning his captains to beware of any activity that would result in confiscation of his vessels. Yet he was certainly not averse to trade with the French; he carried naval stores and provisions to them in considerable quantities and was occasionally so bold as to instruct his captains to trade with British islands only as a last resort.[16]

Court, File Papers, Sept., 1741–Dec., 1743, 7 vols., 6:56; Andrew Burnaby, *Burnaby's Travels Through North America*, 3d ed., ed. Rufus R. Wilson (New York: A. Wessels, 1904), p. 93; Chambers Russel to Governor Greene, July 8, 1748, *RICR*, 5:258–59; John Banister to John Steadman, February 27, 1748, Banister Letterbook, 1748, p. 218; *Boston Gazette*, June 14, 1748; Christopher Champlin to Thomas Remington, December 15, 1759, Champlin Papers, box 4, folder F; John Banister to Anthony Soulard, June 20, 1748, Banister Letterbook, 1748–50, p. 30; *Petitions*, 6:152; Samuel Ward to Henry Ward, February 20, 1758, Ward MS., box 1, RIHS, p. 36; *RICR*, 6:173–74, 218–19, 252–53; *Notary Records*, 7:119, 241, 324.

[15]Hazard took the added precaution of flying French colors when he sailed into the harbor, and he carried three Frenchmen on board as well. When captured by a British privateer, he tried to pretend that he was just a passenger on the sloop. *Equity Court*, 6:56.

[16]James Duncan to Metcalf Bowler and Co., February 1760, Champlin Papers, box 4, folder D; James Duncan to Christopher Champlin and Co., September 1758, Champlin Papers (Bound), 1:67, RIHS; James Duncan to Christopher Champlin and Co., February 14, 1760, *Commerce of Rhode Island*, p. 85; Howard Preston, *Rhode Island and the Sea* (Providence: State of Rhode Island and Providence Plantations, Office of the Secretary of State, 1932), p. 63; Beer, *British Colonial Policy*, p. 103 and n.; Christopher Champlin to Peter James, November 20, 1744, Champlin Papers, box 4, folder I; John Banister and Moses Lopez to Capt. Thomas Rodman, April 27, 1748,

One point remains clear about Newport's trade with the enemy in time of war. Rhode Island was singled out, probably unfairly, as the most notorious of His Majesty's wayward colonies. At the end of the War of Austrian Succession, stories of illegal trade were thoroughly investigated, and the British government was both angered and humiliated by the blatant violations that had occurred.[17] By 1761, Joseph Sherwood, the London agent for the colony, was warning Governor Hopkins of the "great disgust" with which influential Englishmen viewed such activity. And in 1762, the worst suspicions of Englishmen appeared confirmed when General Jeffery Amherst seized papers from a group of Frenchmen who had come to America to establish commercial relations with the colonies. According to Amherst, the papers indicated that "Rhode Island is one of the principle [*sic*] colonies on which [the French] depend; and that Several of the merchants of Newport are deeply concerned in this iniquitous trade."[18]

Reports like those of General Amherst seemed plausible, for there was other disagreeable news concerning Newport that found its way to London. Governor William Shirley of Massachusetts constantly accused the city of being a willing haven for deserters from other colonies. And while agent Richard Partridge had defended Newport against the aspersions cast upon it in the 1740s, Rhode Island

John Banister to Capt. James Brown, December 10, 1748, Banister Letterbook, 1748–50, pp. 2, 161, 168. Pardon Tillinghast also dealt with Frenchmen in a manner that "Required Secrecy and Dispatch." *Equity Court*, 7:54.

[17]See Frank W. Pitman, *The Development of the British West Indies, 1700–1763* (New Haven: Yale University Press, 1917), app. 2, for the investigations of Rhode Island's illegal trade during the War of Austrian Succession. Massachusetts helped fuel the flames of hostility when it accused Rhode Island officials of contributing less than their share to the Louisbourg expedition. Richard Partridge to Friend William Sharpe, July 22, 1745, *Letters to the Governors*, 2:150.

[18]Joseph Sherwood to Governor Hopkins, May 30, 1761, in Kimball, *Correspondence*, 2:320; General Amherst to the Governor of Rhode Island, May 7, 1762, and General Amherst to Governor Hopkins, April 15, 1762, *RICR*, 6:318, 312.

incurred once more the special displeasure of the mother country.[19] Damaged relations with Britain were made even worse when members of the Royal Navy suffered mob violence in Newport streets. Inhabitants and transients, expressing their disapproval of unpopular British policies that properly elected city officials seemed helpless to change, occasionally gathered to "obstruct, insult, assault" and "abuse" naval officers suspected of having impressment on their minds. Wartime activity did nothing to improve relationships between British officials and the town of Newport and indeed did much to harm them.[20]

While tales of Newport's disregard of British imperial policy and disruption of the war effort were exaggerated, they had their effect nevertheless. They encouraged London's determination to suppress illegal trade, thus further reducing the chances for successful activity. Consequently, illicit trade became more hazardous, if not invariably less profitable, as the wars of the mid-eighteenth century dragged on.

The most serious difficulties appeared during the Seven Years' War. As hostilities were renewed after 1755, merchants at first assumed that trade with the enemy would be no more difficult than in the past. While risks were always a component of such activity, many of Newport's commercial leaders felt that potential profits made it well worth the trouble. Indeed, in June 1757 the Rhode Island assembly frankly admitted that its efforts to stop the French trade were futile, and despite repeated attempts by the colony government to thwart it, the government was helpless in face of the town's wily seamen. But in the end Newport's merchant adventurers were seriously crippled if not destroyed. They were thwarted not by the colonial government but by forces over which they exercised no control.[21]

[19]*RICR*, 5:107; 6:186, 187, 154; Richard Partridge to the Governor of Rhode Island, May 3, 1745, *Letters to the Governors*, 2:140.

[20]*RICR*, 6:52; Andrew Stone to the Governor of Rhode Island, October 1, 1743, in Kimball, *Correspondence*, 1:237.

[21]*RICR*, 6:6, 11–12, 58, 147–48, 442–43; 5:425, 517.

With the start of the Seven Years' War, the British West Indies began to compete for their share of the French trade, using the time-honored methods of flags of truce and trade through neutral ports. The islands were challenging Newport merchants at their own game—and they were winning! The odds were distinctly in favor of the island traders, for their vessels were often accompanied by British men-of-war who gave them protection from French privateers, protection seldom afforded to Newport vessels. The city's merchants bitterly protested this policy, claiming that they, who contributed generously to the war effort, were being treated like poor cousins, while the West Indies planters who had sacrificed practically nothing in the war were being helped. Nevertheless, competition from West Indian vessels continued, disturbing trading conditions that were always unstable, even in the best of times. Those Newport vessels fortunate enough to make it safely to Monte Cristi were confronted with chronically glutted markets and high prices. Captain William Grant's complaint that "as for times here they are so bad I don't care to say anything about it" was not exaggerated. Competition from other American colonies increased pressure on French markets. Everyone, it seemed, was getting into the act. In 1761, George Champlin complained that the price of molasses in Monte Cristi, that "dreary hole," was "most shocking." He had nothing worth exchanging there but horses and tobacco, as vessels from Philadelphia had already glutted the market with flour and other provisions.[22]

Newport merchants were not confronted merely with unfair competition from the West Indies, but their unprotected vessels were increasingly subject to hostile attacks from the British navy,

---

[22]Burnaby, *Travels*, p. 129; *Newport Mercury*, January 16, 1759; William Grant to Christopher Champlin, November 28, 1759, and April 20, 1760, *Commerce of Rhode Island*, pp. 79, 82; George Champlin to Metcalf Bowler and Christopher Champlin, February 14, 1761, Champlin Papers, box 4, folder C. See also Capt. John Remington to Champlin and William Lister, March 23, 1760, ibid., folder D; John Livingston to Christopher Champlin, August 18, 1758, ibid., folder E; and Richard Oliver to Abraham Redwood, August 24, 1760, *Commerce of Rhode Island*, p. 84.

from West Indian vessels, and from French privateers and men-of-war. Even the legal trade to Monte Cristi and other ports was endangered. Consider the case of Christopher Champlin's schooner *Chance*, which in October 1759 was returning with proper clearances from Hispaniola but was captured by an English man-of-war and sent to Jamaica. The vessel managed to escape from its first captor but was immediately taken by a French privateer, which confiscated the schooner and its cargo.[23]

Trade with the enemy through the use of flags of truce also became more hazardous after 1755. In 1748, John Banister had reflected the optimism of many merchants when he wrote to John Steadman: "The sweets of the French Trade by way of flags of Truce has put me upon turning my Navigation that way which is the most profitable business I know of." But during the Seven Years' War, the sweets were turning sour, and an always hazardous trade became even more "uncertain and strongly Checker'd." Plagued by both increasing competition from the West Indies and the more vigilant surveillance of British men-of-war, Newport merchants faced a most discouraging scene.[24]

While unfriendly observers gave their greatest attention to the illicit trade that occupied many Newport merchants between 1740 and 1765, it is probably true that most commercial affairs were

[23]Governor Hopkins to Secretary Pitt, December 20, 1760, *RICR*, 6:265; George Champlin to Metcalf Bowler and Christopher Champlin, February 14, 1761, Champlin Papers, box 4, folder C; *Newport Mercury*, January 16, 1759, October 19, 1762; *Notary Records*, 7:passim; Captain Duncan to Christopher Champlin, October 1759, Champlin Papers, box 4, folder F; John Livingston to Christopher Champlin, April 7, 1760, ibid., folder D; William Lister to Christopher Champlin, December 13, 1758, ibid., folder E; David Jamison to Christopher Champlin, July 3, 1760, *Commerce of Rhode Island*, p. 83.

[24]John Banister to John Steadman, February 27, 1748, Banister Letterbook, 1748, p. 218; James Duncan to Metcalf Bowler and Co., February 1760, Champlin Papers, box 4, folder D; James Duncan to Christopher Champlin and Co., September 1758, Champlin Papers (Bound) 1:67; James Duncan to Christopher Champlin and Co., February 14, 1760, *Commerce of Rhode Island*, p. 85.

conducted along the same lines and with essentially the same methods as they had been earlier in the century. This trade also was made more tenuous by war. All of the city's commercial leaders saw their trade suffering from more than the usual share of dislocations and nightmarish uncertainties. While some saw opportunity, others met disaster; there was constant insecurity and anxiety for all. Thus each merchant, depending on his circumstances, his needs, and his assets, strove in his own way to cut losses and protect his position.

Not all of the losses suffered in this period could be attributed to wartime conditions. Many if not most setbacks resulted from the routine accidents that plagued seafarers in the eighteenth century, and the more affluent entrepreneur could generally expect and absorb an occasional loss sustained in this manner. Other losses, however, could not be written off so easily. In wartime, merchants could never be sure that their ships would be allowed to leave port. Embargoes could be laid on vessels carrying provisions, and the ships or provisions were sometimes commandeered by the government if they were needed for the war effort. Some merchants lived in constant fear that their privateers would be impressed for transporting colony troops.[25] Once vessels left port, moreover, they risked being taken by the enemy's "marauding sloops," which lingered near Newport's harbor despite the best efforts of the colony sloop *Tartar* to deter them. The threat from other vessels continued throughout a voyage. Seven Newport vessels resting near Jamaica were taken by the Spanish in the summer of 1743. In 1758, one French frigate burned seven Newport ships and carried two more away as prizes; all nine were laden with valuable sugar and molasses. Indeed the notarial records of this period are replete with accounts of

[25]*Boston Gazette*, December 16, 1746, January 9, 1753; *Newport Mercury*, May 11, 1762, April 14, 1764; David Lindsay to Capt. Phillip Wilkinson, June 19, 1753, in George Mason, *Reminiscences of Newport* (Newport: Charles E. Hammet, Jr., 1884), MS. ed., 2:80, NHS; *Notary Records*, 6:64, 252, 276; *RICR*, 5:444–45, 6:40; Metcalf Bowler to Christopher Champlin, 1757, Champlin Papers, box 4, folder G.

Newport vessels attempting to carry on normal, perfectly legal, commercial operations—and suffering capture by the French.[26]

The wars of the mid-eighteenth century created other problems for Newport merchants. Since even a relatively small supply of goods could glut any market, communication between factors, owners, and captains was essential. But the hazards of war often made it impossible for letters to cross the open seas unimpeded. Businessmen constantly complained that the lack of information about markets and supplies made ventures riskier than ever. Even when they sent their correspondents "Triplicates of every Letter (. . . during the Continuance of War)," they often failed to prevent captains from sailing into crowded ports where prices for their goods plummeted while the cost of sugar and molasses was being driven up by as much as 25 percent. This disruption of trade occurred in time of peace as well as war, but there is no doubt that poor communications, resulting in failed trading voyages, made ventures especially hazardous when the mother country was engaged in imperial conflicts.[27]

Direct trade with London also suffered as a result of war. Ships were often forced to wait in the colonies for convoys before they could depart. On the way to London, vessels easily strayed from convoys and were often taken by the enemy. Under such circumstances insurance rates between England and the American colonies were prohibitive. John Tomlinson frequently warned Abraham Redwood to divide the goods he sent to London among at least three vessels as long as the war lasted. William Stead had difficulty sending goods from London to Christopher Champlin in the fall of 1756 because so few vessels were departing from Rhode Island.

[26]*Boston Gazette*, June 30, 1740, August 2, 1743; *Newport Mercury*, January 23, 1759; *Notary Records*, 6, 7:passim.

[27]Joseph Sherwood to Stephen Hopkins, May 30, 1761, *Letters to the Governors*, 6:51; Thomas Remington to Christopher Champlin and Co., March 15 and 23, 1760, Champlin Papers, unbound box (1732–1800), RIHS.

Stead blamed the renewed hostilities with France for this state of affairs.[28]

Even when allowances are made for the tendency of many merchants to dwell on their liabilities while ignoring their assets, it is apparent that for many entrepreneurs, trading conditions in this period had taken on a nightmarish quality. The expenses of war, a severe drought in 1762, a gravely dislocated system of trade, and the chronic lack of specie all worked together to give the entire town "a most gloomy aspect." Before the Seven Years' War had ended, at least four merchants had petitioned the general assembly for permission to declare bankruptcy, asserting that any efforts to pay their arrears while languishing in debtors' prison would be as if "to remove mountains and throw them into the Midst of the Sea." Jacob Roderiguez Riviera narrowly avoided financial ruin by using the Insolvency Act and unlimited credit, and Godfrey Malbone's sons were also "losing greatly in trade." Even Henry Collins, once described as the "Lorenzo de Medici of Newport," faced economic disaster, as he was forced into bankruptcy and had to sell his property to George Rome, a much vilified member of Newport's incipient Loyalist community.[29]

The adverse economic effects of war were not limited to the merchants. Small businessmen in Newport were also plagued by

[28]John Banister to Capt. Benjamin Turner, April 30, 1748, Banister Letterbook, 1748–50, p. 4; Crawford, Sloop *Roby;* Robert Plumstead to Samuel Ayrault, October 6, 1757, Ayrault Letters, bk. 2, 1:43, NHS; John Tomlinson to Abraham Redwood, March 18, 1744/45, *Commerce of Rhode Island*, p. 51; William Stead to Christopher Champlin, September 6, 1756, Champlin Papers, box 4, folder M; Stephen Greenleaf to Christopher Champlin, January 25, 1745, ibid., folder I.

[29]Henry Ward to Samuel Ward, February 28, 1758, Ward MS., box 1, p. 36; Governor Ward to Joseph Sherwood, August 6, 1762, in Kimball, *Correspondence*, 2:336; Samuel Ward to Lords of Trade and Plantations, November 19, 1765, Ward MSS., box 1, p. 59; *Newport Mercury*, January 10 and February 28, 1763, and September 10 and October 22, 1764, and 1765, passim; Henry Cruger to Aaron Lopez, September 4, 1765, *Commerce of Rhode Island*, p. 118; *Petitions*, 9:102; Mason, *Reminiscences*, p. 58; Samuel Ward to Anna Ward, January 14, 1765, Ward MSS., box 1, p. 51; John Callender, *An Historical Discourse of the Civil and Religious Affairs of the Colony of Rhode Island*, 2d rev. ed. (Providence: Knowles, Vose, 1838), p. 44 n.

uncertainty in this period, as their symbiotic relationship with commercial capital tied their prosperity inextricably to the prosperity of the merchant community. When trade was depressed, their businesses were hurt. Commercial decline meant tight money and reduced buying power for all consumers. It also meant that supplies from abroad were less plentiful, and those goods that were brought into the harbor were often sold at exorbitant prices. Credit also became tighter, for as merchant creditors in London began to demand payment on their loans, Newport merchants in turn demanded immediate payment from shopkeepers, most of whom had bought wholesale goods on the assumption that they would be given at least six months to pay for them. This situation forced artisans to sell their goods for "ready cash" or, if need be, for short credit only. When money grew tighter, construction in the once bustling city ground to a halt: between 1750 and 1760, not one house a year was built there. This decline not only reflected the stagnant economy but contributed to the general downward spiral as well.[30]

The policies of Great Britain inadvertently contributed to the short money supply. While the British had promised the colony that its heavy wartime expenses would be reimbursed "to a shilling," in fact during and after both major wars of the period the Lords tended to "Spin out their time" whenever the subject was broached by colonial agents. As late as 1765, Governor Ward was still trying to obtain money promised by British authorities. The reluctance of the British government to honor its commitments was particularly harmful, as Ward pointed out, for "there never was a Time when the Colony had more need of Relief from home." Newport, he said, suffered under an "amazing load of Debt," contracted in part when

---

[30]James Woodcocke to Abraham Redwood, April 4, 1740, Redwood Letters, bk. 644, 1:68, NHS; *Equity Court*, 6:15–16, and 1:21; Morris A. Gutstein, *The Story of the Jews of Newport: Two and a Half Centuries of Judaism, 1658–1908* (New York: Bloch, 1936), p. 67; Caroline E. Robinson, *The Hazard Family of Rhode Island 1635–1894* (Boston: For the Author, 1895), p. 8; *RICR*, 5:267–68, 318, 376; Edmund S. Morgan, *The Gentle Puritan: A Life of Ezra Stiles, 1727–1795* (New Haven: Yale University Press, 1962), p. 112.

the colony helped the mother country in its greatest need. It seemed only fair that London should return the favor now that the colonists were experiencing their own difficulties.[31]

Once again, the effects of the wartime economy were felt unevenly, and not all artisans and shopkeepers failed. But the threat of failure and the relative lack of control over their fortunes were apparent to all. One economic analyst astutely explained the situation in 1754. Trade, he declared, was like a game of nine pins. Only one pin might be struck by some economic calamity, but if one fell others were sure to follow. "All are shook, but some by Chance stayed out the Game. But, are those that stand, better Pins than those that fall?" He thought not. In the years during and immediately after the wars of the mid-eighteenth century, many "pins" were falling. Even a glance at the pages of the *Newport Mercury* after 1760 shows that many small businessmen were forced to declare bankruptcy.[32]

The end of the war did not bring much immediate relief to the merchants, artisans, and shopkeepers of Newport. Postwar depression, a new and tighter British imperial policy, stronger economic and political competition from the mainland city of Providence (made possible partly by the wartime dislocations Newport faced), and the emergence of a Loyalist faction during the Stamp Act crisis (dividing the city's political leadership and making the Stamp Act riots more explosive), all contributed to the malaise after 1763.

[31]Peter Warren to Governor Wanton, September 13, 1745, *RICR*, 5:144–45; Richard Partridge to the Governor of Rhode Island, February 24, 1746/47, in Kimball, *Correspondence*, 2:46; Joseph Harrison to Samuel Ward, June 29, 1762; Report to Lords of the Treasury on Petition of Joseph Sherwood, January 19, 1761, *Letters to the Governors*, 6:90, 43; Richard Partridge to Governor Hopkins, February 12, 1756, in Kimball, *Correspondence*, 2:186–87; Samuel Ward to Joseph Sherwood, May 17, 1765, Ward MSS., box 1, p. 54; Samuel Ward to Joseph Sherwood, August 6, 1762, *Letters from the Governors*, 1:129.

[32][Anonymous,] *The Ill Policy and Inhumanity of Imprisoning Insolvent Debtors* (Newport: n.p., 1774).

Not all of Newport's commercial leaders reacted in the same way to their common problems. Some began investing in industry; others turned to real estate; still others tried to put some distance between themselves and their provincial mercantile affairs by securing place, patronage, and prestige through powerful friends in London. They were willing, said one critic, "to sacrifice their own honour and their country's interest and bend the knee to an unworthy favorite or minister, for a paltry place or pension."[33]

Most merchants continued their trading activities, trying every political and economic trick in the book—much of which was still being written by Newport entrepreneurs—to help themselves through hard times. But some were so distressed by events of the past decades that they turned away from trade altogether. Thomas Chesbrough, for example, retired to his country estate and admonished his brother David: "never take risks . . . when you have a Landed Estate, have no Concern with the Sea. With Diligence and Frugality, your Estate will increase fast eno' without exposing it to Hazard." And John Banister, whose taste for the "art and Mistery" of commercial affairs was nearly all consuming, warned his son Thomas against becoming involved in mercantile activity, telling him that he had "arising out of the profits of his Estate Sufficient Competency with the Blessing of a kind Providence and frugal management to Support him and a family," and thus he would be wise "not to Enter into trade."[34]

But these men were exceptional. While Newport merchants admitted that the economy had fallen in a slump aggravated by Britain's new imperial policy, they never lost their optimistic faith in the future. By 1767, with the partial repeal of the Sugar Act, the repeal of the Stamp Act, the rapid growth of the whaling industry, and the opening of new opportunities in the slave trade, many

[33]Ezra Stiles, *The Literary Diary of Ezra Stiles*, 2 vols., ed. Franklin B. Dexter (New York: Charles Scribner's Sons, 1901), 1:39, 270.

[34]Ezra Stiles, *Itineraries and Correspondence of Ezra Stiles, 1755–1794*, ed. Franklin B. Dexter (New Haven: Yale University Press, 1916), p. 1; *New England Historical and Genealogical Record* 69 (1915): 223.

thought that good times would shine on Newport once more. However, Newport's commercial future was destined to be at least as "uncertain and strongly Checker'd" as its recent past. The events of the 1750s and 1760s should have served as a warning that the economic future of the city was not assured, that British policy and Newport's needs were not always complementary, and that the next crisis might be even greater. Wars had disrupted the urban economy, damaged relations between Newport and the mother country, and shown colonial merchants that their much vaunted economic prosperity was based on a very shaky foundation. By 1776, Newport's commercial dominance had ended. Never again would the town be able to proclaim its central importance to the material welfare of Rhode Island. Never again could it hope to supplant Boston or New York as a major center of trade. Perhaps John Banister and Thomas Chesbrough had been correct in advising their relatives to avoid risk, avoid the sea, and avoid trade.

Born of War, Killed by War: The Company of Military Adventurers in West Florida

ROBIN F. A. FABEL

*T*he starting point for the tale of the Company of Military Adventurers is 1763, a year of muted triumph for the British. Those of us who can remember 1945 may see a parallel. After years of defeat, danger, struggle, and draining expense, the British Empire had emerged victorious from the ordeal of war. Skeptics saw flaws in the imperial structure. Hindsight makes us pay particular attention to them, but we should remember that there were others, optimists, who foresaw no disintegration, who found it difficult to believe that the sense of unity and cooperation fostered by war would not endure in the postwar years. Winston Churchill, in one of his most famous speeches of the 1940s, spoke of the British Empire as possibly lasting a thousand years. In 1763 there were Americans of similar stamp. They had helped to defeat the traditional French and Spanish enemies and were proud of it. Completely confident of the continued expansion and prosperity of the empire, they looked to profit from the rewards of victory. Of such was the Company of Military Adventurers.

Their leader was Phineas Lyman, who was, as far as the British were concerned, the most distinguished American to take part in what Lawrence Gipson has called the Great War for Empire. Whether or not the description is accurate, Lyman was certainly more highly esteemed by the British than was young Colonel George Washington. Lyman was appointed major general in command of all Connecticut forces as early as 1755, and he served ably in seven campaigns during the war, culminating in the successful siege of Havana in 1762, where he commanded all American provincial troops.

His British superiors, the earl of Albemarle and General Jeffery Amherst, encouraged Lyman to establish a settlement in the western colonies with discharged soldiers and no doubt promised him that they would use their influence in England to see that he and his New Englanders were treated generously.[1] This organization of war veterans, called the Company of Military Adventurers, first met in Hartford, Connecticut, on June 15, 1763. Each adventurer paid two dollars to finance a trip to England for Lyman.[2] With several specific goals in mind, all of which had the general aim of securing compensation for wartime sacrifice and prowess, he was to lobby the British government.

The ministry acted with uncommon dispatch. The well-known Proclamation Act of October 7, 1763, authorized grants of free land to veterans according to a graduated scale ranging from 5,000 acres for a field officer to 50 acres for a private soldier. The proclamation forbade settlement west of the Alleghenies, except in the new British colony of West Florida.[3] This huge province was almost without European population. It embraced sizable parts of four modern states: Florida, Alabama, Louisiana, and Mississippi. It was a significant exception, and, if the arguments of outraged land speculators who had invested further north could be ignored, sufficient in area to accommodate westward immigration for some time to come.

Superficially what Lyman had sought in England had been achieved, but, with reason, he tarried. He wanted to ensure that

[1]Benjamin W. Dwight, *The History of the Descendants of John Dwight of Dedham, Massachusetts* (New York: J. F. Trow and Son, 1874), 121–22.

[2]*Providence Gazette*, January 3, 1773.

[3]Arthur Berriedale Keith, ed., *Selected Speeches and Documents on British Colonial Policy, 1763–1917* (London: Oxford University Press, 1933), 1:3–11.

provincials, as opposed to regular British soldiers, were also included in the royal bounty, for the wording of the Proclamation Act had been vague on this point.[4] Lyman tried in vain to obtain a ruling from the king as some colonial governors did exclude provincial veterans as ineligible. Seldom mentioned as a cause of prerevolutionary discontent, this discrimination harmed thousands of Americans in the 1760s and 1770s. George Washington's application for land in West Florida, for example, was rejected by Governor Peter Chester because Washington was not an officer in the regular British forces.[5]

Lyman also stayed in England to ensure that the boundary of West Florida was extended northward to include the lush Mississippi lands around Natchez, an alteration that was made in 1764; although in this instance the most effective lobbying came from the first governor of West Florida, who was then waiting to take up his appointment.[6] But Lyman continued to wait in England. He asked for a huge tract of 150,000 acres to be allocated specifically to the Company of Military Adventurers, and he even aspired to the creation of a new and separate colony on the banks of the Mississippi: perhaps he liked the thought of being governor.[7] If so, he was quite out of luck because Lord Hillsborough, the secretary of state for America, firmly opposed new inland colonies. Lyman did receive as consolation a personal tract of 20,000 acres, which he was allowed to locate anywhere he chose within the borders of West Florida.[8] Unappeased by this sop, the general seemed fully persuaded that the only bar to the realization of his hopes for the

[4]Great Britain, Public Record Office, London, Colonial Office Papers 5/630, Memorial of Major Timothy Hierlihy and others to the West Florida Council, March 5, 1774.

[5]George Washington to Thomas Lewis, February 17, 1774, in John C. Fitzpatrick, ed., *The Writings of George Washington* . . . (Washington, D.C.: Government Printing Office, 1931–44), 3:184.

[6]Clarence Carter also thought that land speculators close to the ministry, like the Earl of Eglinton and Thomas Robinson, were influential in effecting the boundary change. Clarence E. Carter, "Some Aspects of British Administration in West Florida," *Mississippi Valley Historical Review* 1 (1914–15): 368.

[7]*New York Journal*, January 21, 1768.

[8]CO 5/607:216–19.

military adventurers was Hillsborough's continued tenure in office. Finally, as soon as the secretary resigned in August 1772, Lyman sailed for America.

It was entirely understandable that he should return; he had squandered nine years in Britain and was no longer young. If he were to bring a pioneer community into existence, his time was short; as long ago as 1767, he had talked to Benjamin Franklin of leading his people into the wilderness if the ministry did not give him what he wanted.[9] Besides, by the early 1770s the government was more concerned with holding on to existing American colonies than with starting new ones.

General Lyman affected jubilation on his return to New England. He alleged that the ministry had agreed to allocate the 150,000 acres he had sought. He was believed, although he possessed no document to back his assertion. An excited group of revivified adventurers met at the Hartford courthouse on November 18, 1772. They elected Lyman their leader with the title of moderator, and they appointed a nine-man committee to explore the Mississippi valley to find a suitable uninhabited tract. Among memorable committee members were Colonel Israel Putnam and Lyman's son Thaddeus. To charter a boat and pay their expenses, the company launched a new drive for membership, which was widened to embrace nonveterans prepared to pay substantially for the privilege.[10] With an admirable lack of delay, the explorers sailed on December 19, 1772, aboard the sixty-five-ton sloop *Mississippi*. On February 28, 1773, they reached Pensacola, where local luminaries made the committee welcome.[11]

West Florida was still, after ten years of existence, an underpopulated colony. Moreover it had attracted a great many riffraff described by a former governor as "the overflowing scum of all other

[9]Benjamin Franklin to William Franklin, June 13, 1767, in Clarence W. Alvord and Clarence E. Carter, eds., *Illinois Historical Collections* (Springfield: Illinois State Historical Library, 1916), 11:574.

[10]*Providence Gazette*, January 30, 1773.

[11]Albert C. Bates, ed., *The Two Putnams, Israel and Rufus, in the Havana Expedition and in the Mississippi River Exploration, 1772–73 with some Account of the Company of Military Adventurers* (Hartford: Connecticut Historical Society, 1931), pp. 143, 155.

societies." [12] Clearly the adventurers were different and were considered a better class of people. They were not out to make a quick Spanish dollar through illicit trade before migrating elsewhere. They were solid New England worthies intent on farming, attracted by good economic prospects, fleeing not from the law but from an unhappy economic situation.

In the early 1770s it was not necessary to face the excruciating dilemma of siding with or opposing rebellion. Economic motives sufficiently explain why thousands of Connecticut men and women contemplated leaving their settled colony for the fevers and hardships of the Mississippi wilderness. Next to Rhode Island, Connecticut was the most densely populated American colony: between 1762 and 1774 its population rose by 50,000. The soil of Connecticut had been worn out by incessant cropping and backward farming techniques. Average acreage was small, and obtaining more was difficult. Much of the arable land was of unreachably high price or held by absentee landlords for speculation. Emigration in all directions was common—in the late 1760s, it averaged 2,000 persons per year. The prospects for a small farmer, especially one with a large family, were much better on the rich Mississippi lands advertised by the military adventurers. [13]

Governor Chester was cordial to the exploring committee, although he regretted that he had received no instructions authorizing the grant of any specific tract of land to the military adventurers. Of course he was prepared to recognize General Lyman's documented personal grant of 20,000 acres. He advised the explorers not to waste the favorable spring weather by delaying in Pensacola but rather to explore up the Mississippi River, marking out future townships on

[12]George Johnstone to the Earl of Halifax, June 11, 1765, in Dunbar Rowland, ed., *Mississippi Provincial Archives, 1763–1768, English Dominion* (Nashville: Press of Brandon Printing Co., 1911), 1:257.

[13]Oscar Zeichner, *Connecticut's Years of Controversy, 1750–1776* (Chapel Hill: University of North Carolina Press, 1949), pp. 143–45. See also an anonymous letter in *New York Journal*, January 7, 1773, for contemporary testimony to the economic lure of the Mississippi.

its eastern shore in the far northwest of the province. By the time they returned to Pensacola, it was probable that official approval for their land grant would have arrived.[14]

Exploration proved tediously slow. It took the sloop *Mississippi* two weeks to get as far as New Orleans, where the lieutenant-governor of West Florida lent the explorers a barge. They used oars to toil upstream until April 26, when they reached the fort at Natchez, the most northerly British settlement in West Florida. Encountering many rival settlers around Natchez, they pushed on even further north to the banks of the Bayou Pierre and the Big Black River, where the only objectors were the Choctaw Indians, who were fearful of losing their traditional hunting grounds.[15] As men of their time, the New Englanders were insensitive to well-founded Indian fears that their way of life was threatened, and they ignored General Lyman's belief that settlement should be attempted only in cooperation with the Indians.[16] Rejoining the *Mississippi* after surveying the land favorably and having adventures too numerous to mention here, the explorers were back in Pensacola by the beginning of July. They had earmarked nineteen sites suitable for townships, and Elias Durnford, the surveyor general of West Florida, placed the sites on a map. Although still uninformed of a grant from London for the adventurers, the provincial council seemed determined to indulge them as much as the law would allow and agreed to reserve the townships, each comprising 23,000 acres, until March 1, 1774, with a further extension of time if proof were provided of adventurer families actively preparing to leave for the Mississippi valley.

Encouraged by the explorers' report, some four hundred members of the Company of Military Adventurers, each the head of a household, met in Hartford on November 3, 1773, and ordered the immediate sailing of emigrant vessels to West Florida.[17] The old

[14]CO 5/630:Council Minutes, March 5, 1773.

[15]Bates, *Two Putnams*, pp. 192, 202–03.

[16]Phineas Lyman, "Reasons for a settlement on the Mississippi, 1766," *Illinois Historical Collections* 11:265–89.

[17]Bates, *Two Putnams*, p. 44.

Mississippi left New Haven on December 17 with about fifty passengers. Another sloop, the *Adventurer*, left two days later, also with fifty passengers, including General Lyman and members of his family; they reached Pensacola on March 3, 1774.[18] The company's leaders presented a memorial to Chester, reminding him of his earlier encouragement. Chester was in a quandary, for since the first arrival of the explorers he had received no instructions to give them 150,000 acres of land, but instead he had received a royal order dated April 7, 1773, forbidding land grants except to those qualified under the terms of the 1763 proclamation. Now spurred on partly by his own welcome, there were 104 military adventurer families with an average of seven members each, all highly desirable immigrants, either on their way or actually in West Florida. In these circumstances Chester solved the problem by reversing his usual ban on allowing provincial veterans to have proclamation land. Most of the company leaders could thus qualify. The rest were advised to settle the land as squatters until such time as the ban on land grants was rescinded, as, after two years, it was.[19]

The war that shortly afterward broke out between Britain and the American colonies undoubtedly had a mostly negative effect on this most promising of immigrant schemes. Leaving revolutionary New England for Loyalist West Florida could no longer be regarded as a politically neutral act. In practical terms, too, it became more difficult and dangerous. On the other hand, it incited some New Englanders of Loyalist sympathies, who might not otherwise have done so, to emigrate.

One of these was Major Timothy Dwight, who left Middletown, Connecticut, with other passengers from the Company of Military Adventurers for West Florida as late as May 1776. As a judge in the court of common pleas in Northampton, Massachusetts, for sixteen

[18]Matthew Phelps, *Memoirs and Adventures* (Bennington, Vt.: Press of Anthony Haswell, 1802), p. 16, and app., p. 60.

[19]"The Answer of Governor Chester to the petition of complaint of Adam Chrystie and others," p. 2, Library of Congress, West Florida Papers 74539, reel 4. U.S. National Archives, General Land Office (Division D).

years, Dwight had sworn an oath of loyalty to the British Crown. His refusal to violate it, combined with the threats of the revolutionaries, persuaded him to leave New England.[20] Accompanying him to Florida were two of his sons and his sister Eleanor, the wife of General Lyman.

In effect the adventurers were establishing a new colony. Pensacola, capital of the province they nominally inhabited, was weeks away. As in most pioneer colonies, the mortality rate was high. General Lyman died in September 1774, shortly after his son, Phineas Junior. The general's widow and her brother, Timothy Dwight, died soon after arrival.[21] Their fellow passengers, Jedediah Smith, Mrs. Josiah Flowers, and Mrs. Joseph Leonard, also died in 1776. The husbands of Flowers and Leonard both died in Florida, one at the hands of the Indians. Perhaps most heartrending of all was the story of the family of Matthew Phelps, the only military adventurer to write memoirs. When Phelps reached Manchac on the Mississippi his daughter Abigail and his son Atlantic died of fever. His wife followed them into death a few weeks later. Phelps pressed on with his two surviving children, but they died when a whirlpool on the Big Black River caught the canoe in which their father was hauling them.[22] In spite of misfortunes in most families like the Dwights, Lymans, and Phelpses, there was usually at least one survivor who would not abandon hope and who went on to farm the land. Then the revolutionary war, from which no doubt many of the adventurers had congratulated themselves on escaping, came to West Florida in the shape of Captain James Willing of the United States Navy. With a hundred well-armed followers he floated down the Mississippi in February 1778. Initially the inhabitants of the Natchez district bought freedom from harassment by taking an oath of neutrality and allowing the American flag to rise over Fort Panmure at Natchez. But the leader of the community on the Big

[20]B. Dwight, *Descendants*, pp. 131–34.

[21]Timothy Dwight, *Travels in New England and New York*, ed. Barbara Solomon (Cambridge: Harvard University Press, 1949), 4:225.

[22]Phelps, *Memoirs*, pp. 69–71.

Black and Bayou Pierre, although part of the Natchez district, would not take the oath and gathered supporters who recaptured the Natchez fort for the British. That leader was General Lyman's energetic third son Thaddeus, an undoubted Loyalist who shared command with the like-minded Anthony Hutchins and deployed a scratch force, which vanquished a boatload of Willing's counterattack force in an engagement known as the battle of the White Cliffs.[23] Subsequently a formally approved militia regiment was raised, and Lyman was made captain of one of its companies.[24] The adventurers had survived the first major challenge posed by war chiefly because Willing's intent was raiding rather than permanent occupation. The case was different when the Spanish declared war on Britain in 1779 and from their province of Louisiana on the west bank of the Mississippi attacked the British province across the river. By then the Natchez district had acquired a garrison of British regulars, but the Spanish had the advantage of surprise and skillful leadership. When the British commander at Baton Rouge surrendered, he ceded the entire western half of the province including the Natchez district—to the outrage of inhabitants who refused to accept the verdict. In April 1781, they determined to repossess the Natchez fort, which the Spaniards had garrisoned only lightly. Lacking siege guns, the attackers compelled the Spanish commander to run up the white flag by means of a ruse. It was a bold but ultimately futile Loyalist coup because in the very month that it succeeded the rest of the province of West Florida capitulated to its Spanish conqueror, Bernardo de Gálvez.[25]

Forced into war by its Loyalist leadership, the adventurer community found itself on the losing side. Reluctant to accept Spanish rule, particularly since the capture of the Natchez fort was of dubious legality and may have exposed them to retribution, the

[23]Robert V. Haynes, *The Natchez District and the American Revolution* (Jackson: University Press of Mississippi, 1976), p. 86.

[24]Peter Chester to Lord George Germain, May 7, 1778, CO 5/594:504.

[25]J. F. H. Claiborne, *Mississippi as a Province, Territory and State* (Jackson, Miss.: Power and Barksdale, 1880), pp. 127–29.

leading adventurer families decided on the hazardous course of heading cross-country to the nearest British garrison. Savannah, Georgia, was a good 700 miles away, as the crow flew, but because of hostile Indians and American revolutionaries, a direct route was impossible. The journey was arduous and slow; many of the party were children and infants who fell sick. Their route lay through canebrakes and across mountains and unbridged rivers. The adventurers had to pass through the land of the Choctaws who had not forgiven the encroachment on their hunting grounds. The adventurers journeyed in the sickly southern summer without tents or sufficient provisions. They had only one compass, which soon broke. At one point only the courage of Sereno Dwight enabled them to cross a swift river. At another, when all were dying of thirst, it was his wife Cynthia who found water. Slowly they zigzagged into the Carolinas and then down the Altamaha River; all starving, they dared to enter a Creek village in Georgia. The suspicious braves took them for enemies and would have killed them had not Sereno Dwight used ingenuity and a certain amount of acting ability to persuade the Indians that, like themselves, they were on the Loyalist side in the war.

After this harrowing experience the refugees split into two groups, one of which ran straight into a band of revolutionaries who took them prisoner. The other group moved south of the Altamaha into loyal East Florida and crossed back into Georgia near the coast, safely reaching Savannah after a journey of 1,350 miles and 149 days. There they were joined by their former companions who had been taken prisoner: their American captors had not known what to do with them.[26]

The Company of Military Adventurers had been annihilated, never to rise again. Its members too seemed doomed by their huge and unsuccessful effort. Dynamic leadership had been provided by the Dwights and Lymans, but it is almost as though a curse had been placed on their families. Sereno Dwight joined the British army

---

[26]T. Dwight, *Travels*, 4:214–15, 226–29.

after reaching Savannah. He died at sea in 1782. His widow Cynthia, who had remarried, died in childbirth eight years later. General Lyman's daughters, Eleanor and Experience, both died soon after their arrival in Savannah. Their three surviving brothers, all of whom had settled near the Mississippi as adventurers, joined British forces in Georgia. Thaddeus returned to New England after peace arrived but achieved no distinction; he later deserted his wife and children and ran away to New York. His younger brother Oliver died insane. His other brother, Thompson, disappeared into the obscurity of exile in the Bahamas, where he died young.[27]

Very few of the military adventurers stayed on in West Florida once it became Spanish. The Spanish census of 1792 shows only six such families as still resident in the Natchez district. But being anti-Spanish did not necessarily mean that the Company of Military Adventurers taken as a whole was pro-British, despite the undoubted loyalty of leading families like the Lymans and Dwights. Three of the nine-man exploring committee, for instance, became generals in the Continental forces—Israel Putnam, his cousin Rufus Putnam, and Roger Enos. And the treasurer of the organization, Hugh Ledlie, was the leader of the Sons of Liberty in Connecticut. Most of the adventurers had originated in that colony, fifty out of the sixty-four heads of families that I have identified. The names of no less than thirty-three of the fifty appear in the rolls of Connecticut men who served the American cause in the Revolution.[28] Service in the armed forces does not of itself prove revolutionary fervor, but the return of such a high proportion of adventurers to distant New

[27]B. Dwight, *Descendants*, pp. 215, 219.

[28]Connecticut Historical Society, *Rolls and Lists of Connecticut Men in the Revolution, 1775–1783* (Hartford, 1901), Collections 8: Connecticut General Assembly, *Record of Service of Connecticut Men in the War of the Revolution, the War of 1812 and the Mexican War* (Hartford, 1889); Connecticut Archives, Revolutionary War, Series 1 and 2. For a grant to research in the Connecticut State Archives in the spring of 1980 I am grateful to Auburn University.

England does attest to their disillusionment with what had been a well-organized, ably led, and potentially prosperous immigration scheme. It was war that killed it. Had General Lyman spent three years of lobbying in England, instead of nine, there is every reason to believe that their settlement would have thrived. If the settlements on the Big Black and the Bayou Pierre had been established in the late 1760s, the settled adventurers would surely have been more numerous when war came to the province, and West Florida might have remained British. Alternatively, as a separate state called perhaps Georgiana or Mississippi, its inhabitants might have helped James Willing incorporate the area into the new American republic. The Company of Military Adventurers, which had very much the same life span as the colony of West Florida, originated in British victory in war in 1763 and finally perished about twenty years later in another war.

Good timing was crucial for the fulfillment of Lyman's dream, but in fact the timing of the settlement was fatally awry, chiefly because of needless prevarication by the British government. The founding of a veterans' settlement would have furthered the ends of the empire, but as a result of the delays, the settlement near the Mississippi was too newly planted to acquire sturdiness. It was not the American Revolution that destroyed the company, for on the whole its economically motivated members seem not to have been ideologically divided by or indeed interested in the Revolution. The settlers survived the visit of Willing's marauders in 1778, battered but essentially intact. Some stayed aloof through blatant neutrality. Rather, the Spanish entry into the war polarized the settlers. Staying out of the fight by accepting Spanish rule was an option that almost none took.

The fall of the company through war also meant the extinction of individual reputations. Their heroism, endurance, ingenuity, and sacrifice were not remembered as they most certainly would have been if experienced in the cause of independence. In the end the Spanish conquest of the area settled by the adventurers slowed but did not alter the progress of westward settlement. It was Americans, not Spaniards, who farmed that area, but they were Americans from the back country of Pennsylvania and states farther south. Had the Company of Military Adventurers prospered, the group would have included New Englanders as well.

Pension Expectations
of the French Military Commis

DOUGLAS CLARK BAXTER

Clive Church recently remarked that "the story of the evolution of French central government is in part a search for a reliable set of servants."[1] Historians have been concerned primarily with the struggle between *officier* (officeholder) and *commissaire* (commission holder) in what Roland Mousnier has called a three-hundred-year rivalry culminating in the French Revolution of 1789. Mousnier observed a succession of three types of agents in the evolution of the state: from officeholder to commissioner to modern civil servant (*fonctionnaire*), prefigured in the eighteenth century by the *commis* or clerks in government bureaus. As officeholders acquired ownership with hereditary rights under the system of venality, they became irremovable from office. With a sense of their own importance and essential independence of royal control, corporate groups such as the *parlements* (superior courts) claimed to act as arbitrators between the king and his subjects. The slowness of tradition-bound officeholders during the wars of the seventeenth century led the government to resort to commissioners who represented the person of the king but whose commissions could be revoked at any time. The famed

---

[1]Clive H. Church, *Revolution and Red Tape: The French Ministerial Bureaucracy, 1770–1850* (Oxford: Clarendon, 1981), p. 14.

intendants, other commissioners, the royal council, even governors and ministers represented this appointive principle and were the forces of centralized government.[2]

With the growth of royal authority, the organs of government became formalized. The decline of the chancellery and the conciliar system during the seventeenth and eighteenth centuries led to the concentration of authority in the departments of the control general of finance and the four secretaries of state: foreign affairs, war, marine, and royal household. These offices needed salaried employees to staff their bureaus. In the war department, for example, generals, officeholders, intendants, military commissioners, and others forwarded reports, requests, memoranda, and accounts to the ministry. The war office received and read them, made extracts and copies of important documents, and prepared the paperwork: the commissions, letters, instructions, regulations, and orders. In 1659 Le Tellier had subdivided this work among five bureaus. It became the practice to have a chief clerk, or *premier commis*, to head each bureau and direct several subordinate *commis* as ordinary clerks. As the work of the department grew during the eighteenth century, so did the number of bureaus and the number of *commis*. From 5 in 1659, 7 in 1680, 10 in 1715, to 13 in 1759, the numbers of bureaus, each headed by a *premier commis*, increased. Choiseul reduced the bureaus, and the Comte de Saint-Germain lowered the number again in 1776 to 8. The number of clerks ranged from 54 in 1735, 85

---

[2]Roland Mousnier, "La Fonction publique en France du début du seizième siècle à la fin du dix-huitième siècle. Des officiers aux commissaires puis aux commis, puis aux fonctionnaires," *Revue Historique* 530 (April–June 1979): 321–35. Mousnier has incorporated ideas from this article in his *Institutions de la France sous la monarchie absolue*, vol. 2, *Les Organes de l'État et la Société* (Paris: Presses Universitaires de France, 1980), pp. 81–83 and passim.

In this essay "secretary of state" and "minister" will be used interchangeably, although no secretary was entitled to be called a minister unless the king called him to the *conseil d'en haut*.

in 1745, 180 in 1771, to 105 in 1776, thanks to Saint-Germain's efforts.[3]

During the long administration of the Le Tellier family, the bureaus had all the hallmarks of a fidelity system whereby "creatures" served the interest of their master, who rewarded them through his influence and position, and whose relationship was characterized also by affection and closeness. Part of the reason for this was that their clients were drawn from relatives and acquaintances. Two of the five *premier commis* who headed the bureaus in 1659 were relatives, while an additional three relatives of Le Tellier later served as *premier commis*. Michel Antoine has reminded us that a greater social distance emerged between master and bureau head and, correspondingly, between *premier commis* and *commis*. Antoine uses 1683, the date of death of Colbert, to signal the end of such patrimonial practices, but the decline of clientage is a far more lengthy and complicated process. Chamillart, war minister from 1701 to 1709, employed four relatives in his department, including two *premier commis* and a son who he hoped would succeed him. By the eighteenth century the bureaus were filled by men of experience, leaving less latitude for a minister to replace an expert by an outsider. However, one still saw confidants, especially personal secretaries, brought into the war department. Rochas served as secretary to the intendancies of Dauphiné, Alsace, and Paris under D'Angervilliers; he entered the war department on his master's

---

[3]The numbers of bureaus and *commis* are derived from the following sources: Louis André, *Michel Le Tellier et l'organisation de l'armée monarchique* (Paris: Félix Alcan, 1906), p. 645. Archives de la Guerre at Vincennes, A¹ 1181, fol. 52, "État des choses des bureaux de la guerre depuis l'année 1680." Mousnier, *Organes de l'État*, pp. 166–67. Jean-Pierre Samoyault, *Les Bureaux du secrétariat d'état des affaires étrangères sous Louis XV* (Paris: Editions A. Pedone, 1971), p. 35, n. 3. Michel Antoine, "L'Entourage des ministres aux XVIIe et XVIIIe siècles," in Michel Antoine et al., *Origines et histoire des cabinets des ministres en France* (Geneva: Librairie Droz, 1975), p. 20. Anne Buot de l'Épine, "Les Bureaux de la guerre à la fin de l'Ancien Régime," *Revue d'histoire de droit français et étranger* 54 (1976): 535, n. 6. Church, *Revolution and Red Tape*, pp. 33–34; see also p. 326, n. 21.

accession to the ministry in 1728. As late as the reign of Louis XVI, D'Avranges, who had served fifteen years as Montbarey's secretary, became head of a bureau in 1779 during Montbarey's tenure as minister.[4]

Despite these holdovers of a clientage system, many historians have argued that gradually during the eighteenth century ministries took on the Weberian characteristics of modern bureaucracy, although it was not until the French Revolution that the crucial transformation took place.[5] Mousnier argues that ministries began to: (1) recruit able men after evidence of competence; (2) have regulations governing the activity of the bureaus; (3) demand discretion, fidelity, and obedience from their agents; (4) provide permanent employment, that is, job security; (5) establish hierarchical ranks, whereby the lower levels were supervised by those above but

---

By the latter part of the eighteenth century there were a number of different ranks of *commis: premier commis, sous-chief, commis principal, commis,* and *apprentice.* See Church, *Revolution and Red Tape,* p. 35, table 1, for an elaborate sketch of the title and ranks used in the French ministries under the directory, which he claims is "broadly comparable" to all periods covered by his study. The papers used here, Y³ 26–31 at Vincennes, commonly use the titles of *premier commis* and *commis,* with a sprinkling of *sous-chiefs* and a few *commis principaux* and secretaries. For simplicity, I have treated them only as heads of bureaus (*premier commis*) and subordinates (ordinary *commis*).

[4]For a general discussion of clientage systems, see Roland Mousnier's first volume of his *Institutions de la France sous la monarchie absolue, Société et État* (Paris: Presses Universitaires de France, 1974), pp. 85–93. On the Le Tellier family clientage system, see Douglas Clark Baxter, "Premier Commis in the War Department in the Latter Part of the Reign of Louis XIV," in *Proceedings of the Western Society for French History* 8 (1981): 81–89. In the same volume is a companion piece by John Rule, "The Commis of the Department of Foreign Affairs Under the Administration of Colbert de Croissy and Colbert de Torcy, 1680–1715," pp. 69–80.

Antoine, "Entourage des ministres," p. 19. André Corvisier, "Clientèles et fidélités dans l'armée française aux XVIIe et XVIIIe siècles," in Yves Durand, ed., *Homage à Roland Mousnier. Clientèles et fidélités en Europe à l'époque moderne* (Paris: Presses Universitaires de France, 1981), pp. 217–18. For Rochas, see his pension file, Y³ 31 Rochas. On Montbarey's appointments, see Buot de l'Épine, "Bureaux de la guerre," pp. 550, 556. Church, *Revolution and Red Tape,* p. 40, has other examples.

[5]Church, *Revolution and Red Tape,* pp. 10–12; and for Weber's definition of bureaucracy see p. 319, n. 21.

subordinates could be promoted; (6) make payment according to rank, although salaries were set relatively low because of the "honor" of public service supplemented by the Crown's gratifications; and (7) provide pensions at retirement.[6]

The work of the *commis* and especially that of the bureau chiefs grew in political importance. Government no longer functioned by numerous councils but by individuals working in their offices, supplied by information from their subordinates. As D'Argenson bitterly put it, "The details entrusted to the ministers are immense. Nothing can be done without them. . . . And if their knowledge is not as extended as their powers, they are forced to leave everything to the *commis* who become masters of affairs, and, by consequence, of the state."[7] Under the direction of the *premier commis*, decisions were drawn up, presented to the secretary of state for signature, and published under the legal fiction of an *arrêt du conseil*, although no council saw them. In Mousnier's words, government passed from judicial administration to executive administration.[8]

Who were these ordinary *commis* and their superiors, the *premier commis?* Clive Church has made a computer analysis of 350 clerks who served between 1771 and 1789. He found that almost all were from an urban background and had little formal education, although a few had legal experience. Information on their social origins was elusive. An extremely small number (three) came from noble families; the vast majority were from administrative families, particularly in the war ministry, where Church found 60 percent had at least one relative in the department; the rest came from minor office-holding families, employees in the royal household, *rentier* and commercial backgrounds. They tended to marry in the same groups. Most entered the department fairly young—39 percent before they were

---

[6]Mousnier, "Fonction publique," pp. 331–32, and idem, *Organes de l'État*, pp. 79–80. Mousnier sees the creation of the *École des Ponts et Chaussées* in 1747 as the date for the creation of a modern civil service.

[7]D'Argenson quoted by Buot de l'Épine, "Bureaux de la guerre," p. 558.

[8]Mousnier, "Fonction publique," pp. 333–34, and idem, *Organes de l'État*, pp. 30–31.

twenty, more if one considers those who entered administrative service before employment as *commis*. Many entered because of a tradition of administrative service, family connections, or patronage. Few *commis* could have been attracted by the career prospects: wages were low, and promotion was slow and very rarely to the highest position. Yet they had secure and lifelong income supplemented by pensions and special awards during and after retirement, and some *premier commis* had opportunity for striking gains. Most ordinary *commis*, however, had little financial resources other than their wages. We know more about the *premier commis* because some became prominent: they acquired letters of nobility for their services, and a number became wealthy. Although Church comments that there was more social homogeneity in the war office than in other departments such as foreign affairs, there was still a clear difference in social standing between *commis* and *premier commis* that was accentuated during the later eighteenth century when the numbers in the department expanded due to war. While almost all *premier commis* had served as *commis*, most *commis* had little prospect for such promotion.[9]

Much of our knowledge of the *commis* comes from the Y^a 26–31, *États de personnel* collection in the Archives de la Guerre at Vincennes, consisting of six boxes of individual pension dossiers dating from 1711 to 1789. Each box contains an alphabetically arranged but unpaged series of folders on bureaucrats in the war ministry. These files are not complete for all *commis* who served, particularly for the early part of the century, nor are they the standardized service records that personnel files contain today. Each folder consists of one to a dozen sheets that include petitions by the *commis*, his relatives, or superiors to the minister of war, supporting memoranda, and sometimes the final product, a brevet awarding a pension during service, a retirement pension, or some gratification. There are no records of how decisions were made—most records bear merely the notation "*bon*" and the amount awarded, although un-

---

[9]Church, *Revolution and Red Tape*, pp. 34–40.

doubtedly the minister played a key role. Almost all petitions were successful, though not always in the amount requested, and the few rejected gave no reason for refusal.

These files offer an interesting view of what the civilian personnel felt were good arguments for their requests rather than (strictly speaking) the attitudes of the administration, although there must have been some overlapping of the two. There were no established regulations for retirement until the Comte de Saint-Germain's set of regulations for the war department in 1776. Article 11 of these regulations fixed the retirement benefits of a *premier commis* on a sliding scale: one-quarter of his salary for less than ten years' service, one-third for between ten and twenty years, and half for over twenty years.[10] Thus, until the reign of Louis XVI, custom rather than written regulation determined treatment, and precedent became an extremely important element in memoranda presented for consideration.

Precedents took various forms. Some *commis* merely remarked in a general manner on what colleagues had received, while others gave examples. Anfossy in 1720 requested the regent to consider that while he had been a *commis* he had received a pension of 400 *livres* in 1686, early in his career. He had then acted as a *commissaire des guerres* making a total of twenty-nine years of service to the department. He noted that the smallest pension accorded to a commissioner had been 1,200 *livres* for retirement, and he urged the duc d'Orléans to accord that amount, "as has been practiced for several of his colleagues." *Commis* De Ville in January of the following year, 1721, asked the regent for a pension of 600 *livres* after fourteen years of work in the department. When the regent had returned to the use of secretaries of state after experimenting with a war council under the abortive *polysynodie* system, there was a reshuffling of personnel in the bureaus and De Ville was unemployed. He noted that all of his colleagues similarly situated had received pensions.[11]

[10]Article 11 of the 1776 regulations, cited in Yᵃ 28 Gambier de Campy, Nicolas-Jean; and in Samoyault, *Bureaux du secrétariat d'état*, p. 196, n. 60.

[11]Yᵃ 26 Anfossy; Yᵃ 28 De Ville.

Charles d'Heu, *premier commis*, asked for a pension while still employed. He argued that he had not been treated as favorably as his predecessor, Gilles Charpentier, who had, he sourly remarked, acquired gratifications, gifts of confiscated goods, letters of nobility, and even the charge of treasurer of the military order of St. Louis—worth 6,000 *livres* in revenue. After Charpentier, his nephew Jossigny had obtained 6,000 *livres* in pension. D'Heu complained that "other heads of the same period have had still more advantageous honors and found themselves with wealth very different from this suppliant."[12]

Precedent even governed special cases. In 1749 Monteil requested a pension so that he could live comfortably in the short time he had remaining (it proved to be four years) because of paralysis of his right side, which required constant nursing. "There are few examples that can be cited that bear on Sieur de Monteil's case because some of those who have been accorded pensions have obtained them as rewards for their services, . . . and others were simple copiers to whom one gave 600 *livres* for retirement." Yet Monteil's argument succeeded in obtaining 1,200 *livres*. Likewise, when *commis* Jaquelin became ill and needed money to cover his medical expenses, the minister was reminded that "it is customary in such cases, My Lord, to aid war *commis*, and there is an infinite number of examples of similar graces accorded for shorter maladies."[13]

Precedent was most often cited in widows' requests, perhaps because there was less tradition behind them. As one clerk commented: "It is a usage constantly followed that when a *premier commis* of whatever department obtains his retirement, the minister under whom he served accords him a pension, of which one always assigns a certain part revertible after his death, be it to his spouse if he is married, be it to a niece, or relatives who keep him company."[14]

There were widows who requested pensions and cited examples of others with husbands of similar rank who had obtained them.

[12]Yᵃ 29 D'Heu.
[13]Yᵃ 30 Monteil; Yᵃ 29 Jaquelin.
[14]Yᵃ 27 Chennevières.

Such names repeated over and over suggest that *commis* families knew how their colleagues were treated and expected the same favors; perhaps there was even a model pension request used for these petitions. In the 1750s, for instance, two widows of *premier commis* asked for pensions. Widow Caron noted that Mesdames Laurent and Marie had obtained 2,000 *livres*, while Widows Briquet and Du Chiron received 3,000. Widow Des Prez listed three of these four names, but substituted La Faye's daughter for Laurent. Widows of simple *commis* used the same expedient, although they could hope for less compensation, usually around 600 *livres*. In 1728 Widow Allain provided examples of three others, Pelletier, Agogué, and Boismaigre, who had received that sum. Widow Marchand in the 1730s asked for half of her husband's salary and cited the same three widows as Allain had done. Another, the wife of Paul Des Ecots, mentioned two of the same three again, although she added Allouard and Viot as well. In 1741 a *premier commis* requested a pension for that same Widow Allouard and noted that Pelletier's husband had "almost the same seniority," rewarded by a pension of 600 *livres* to his widow and daughter.[15]

There were other arguments besides precedents. Monteil's request of 1749 noted that "until now pensions given to *commis* in the war bureaus have been proportional to their merit," and it was common for requests to point out services performed. Certain phrases occur repeatedly in petitions—assiduity, zeal, attention to detail—indicating that the war office expected such characteristics in its clerks. D'Heu noted his "assiduous and uninterrupted service," Alexandre the "ninety years of assiduous and disinterested service" of himself and his father, Pinard his service "with zeal, assiduity, and much work." Allain's widow mentioned that her husband had served "in the bureaus with all the application and disinterestedness possible," while Fumeron spoke of his father's record of work "with the same zeal" as head of a bureau under Chamillart and as intendant

---

[15] Y[a] 26 Caron; Y[a] 27 Des Prez; Y[a] 26 Allain; Y[a] 30 Marchand; Y[a] 27 Des Ecots; Y[a] 26 Allouard.

of the armies. Sometimes *commis* went to their superiors for recommendations, simple statements that a *commis* had been employed for so many years, or more detailed praise. When the widow of an assistant applied for a pension, Briquet called him *"un bon commis"* who had always acquitted himself with the greatest exactitude. Another superior gave the deceased *commis* a similar testimonial, adding, "it is my knowledge that he did not leave more than 600 *livres* of income to his heirs." Yet another lauded Laurens's work as "with much exactitude and assiduity." Alexandre in the early 1740s used almost the same language for Allouard, who had worked "with an assiduity, a zeal, and a disinterestedness" that merited reward.[16]

Another common theme in pension requests was seniority. The documents speak of "the most ancient of all the *commis* of the ministers," "one of the oldest and most ancient *commis* in the bureaus," or "one of the oldest *premier commis* of war." Even Monteil, making a case for exceptional treatment due to paralysis, admitted that only one other *commis* enjoyed 1,800 *livres* of pension, "but he was the most ancient in Sieur Alexandre's bureau."[17] Petitioners almost always mentioned the number of years they had put into the war office. Not all *commis* spent their lives in the bureaus—movement was more frequent among the younger members in lower positions—but anyone who examines the files is struck by the remarkable length of individual service. Individuals could enter the service in their late teens or earlier: the oldest *commis* I have discovered, Michel Marchant, retired at age 79 after 68 years of work—he had entered the bureau of fortifications at age 11 and had become a *premier commis* at 24! Because of nepotism, families could accumulate amazing records of experience. The Alexandres, both *premier commis*, father and son, put in 90 years. Chaila Senior put in 40

---

[16]Y[a] 30 Monteil; Y[a] 29 D'Heu; Y[a] 26 Alexandre; Y[a] 30 Pinard (oncle); Y[a] 26 Allain; Y[a] 28 Fumeron de Verrières; Y[a] 27 Des Ecots; Y[a] 29 Laurent (this is Claude Laurens, however); Y[a] 26 Allouard.

[17]Phrases drawn from Y[a] 26 Allouard; Y[a] 29 D'Heu; Y[a] 30 Michellet de Belairmont; Y[a] 27 Claverie de Bannière, Henry; Y[a] 30 Monteil.

years, his eldest son at least 21, his youngest 39. The Blondeau family, father and two sons as *commis* and another son in the army, compiled 163 years of service: 52 years of the total were contributed by the father, who died at age 80. D'Heu, who retired in 1745, had worked for the war office 57 years, 28 of them as head of one of the principal bureaus. Numerous *commis* put in 30, 40, or 50 years, which they never failed to mention in their pension requests.[18]

Petitions also noted the number of other relatives who had served the king, indicating the eighteenth-century *commis* were still some distance from that concept of a modern civil service based on individual accomplishment. But one should not carry this too far, since the petitions never contain the classic expressions of fidelity in a clientage system, "the gift of self," that one reads in the seventeenth century. Missing are the earlier phrases of *créature, affidé, dévoué, domestique,* even *esclave,* and expressions such as "attaching oneself to someone," or "giving one's self to someone." Yet the concepts of fidelity and clientage lingered, and it remains difficult to draw the line between clientage and simple obligation. A master owed protection to the servant and his relatives; if a family served loyally, they deserved rewards. It was natural for sons of *commis* to mention the service of their fathers, for nephews that of their uncles; it showed family attachment to the department. But one *commis* added that his second wife was the daughter of a *commis* of the chancellor and that her first husband was also *premier commis* of war. Two daughters of Marchant added the names of fifteen relatives who had served the army in some capacity, as military commissioners, engineers, and officers. The Widow Fleury announced that she had three sons who were army officers and that one had been killed on campaign. She had also lost a brother and two cousins. Her list hints

---

[18]Y^a 30 Marchant; Y^a 26 Alexandre; Y^a 27 Chaila (père) (fils aîné) (fils cadet); Y^a 26 Blondeau; Y^a 26 Briquet; Y^a 27 Des Ecots; Y^a 29 Jossigny; Y^a 27 Chennevières; Y^a 28 Fumeron de Verrières; Y^a 31 Ségent; Y^a 31 Vallet; Y^a 29 Le Vasseur (père) (fils); Y^a 30 Noiset; Y^a 30 Pinard (oncle); Y^a 30 Marie. D'Heu and Du Chiron are mentioned in Y^a 31 Rochas.

of desperation, and indeed she was without resources except for 100 *livres* in pension.[19]

Some *commis* spoke of patrons at court, especially members of the royal family. One who had lost his position in disgrace mentioned his family's service to the royal household and noted the support of Madame Sophie, daughter of Louis XV. Blondeau's daughter, who sought to have her mother's pension continued, also claimed the favor of a daughter of the king: "Madame Adelaide is interested in the success of this request." Any relation with the royal family was worth mention: Morand had been *huissier* to Madame Sophie, his wife maid to Madame Victoire. *Commis* De Ville, petitioning the duc d'Orléans in 1721, announced that he was the son of an official of both Madame and of Madame the duchesse d'Orléans; "all of his family were ruined" by the death of the duc de Berry, grandson of Louis XIV. De Ville himself had lost the charge of *gentilhomme servant*, worth 11,000 *livres*. Prominent ladies at court such as Madame de Pompadour, the duchesse de Luynes, and the comtesse de Marsan were also mentioned in pension requests. Such patronage was normal under the ancien régime and affected appointments in all departments.[20]

There remains one more plea found in the requests, and it is difficult to evaluate—financial need. There are no studies of the fortunes of *commis*. We do know that *premier commis* of war received comfortable incomes, although less than those in the foreign affairs office. Their salaries varied according to ability, seniority, and favor of the minister and generally increased during the inflation of the eighteenth century. Salaries of *premier commis* were low at the beginning of the century, 3,000 *livres* or so; but by 1771 marshal de Belle-Isle proposed to set their salaries at 12,000 *livres* a year, and

[19]Yves Durand, "Clientèles et fidélités dans le temps et dans l'espace," in Durand, *Homage*, p. 9. Yᵃ 27 Claverie de Bannière, Henry; Yᵃ 30 Marchant; Yᵃ 28 Fleury. See also Yᵃ 26 Agogué (fils).

[20]Yᵃ 26 Agogué (fils); Yᵃ 26 Blondeau; Yᵃ 30 Morand; Yᵃ 28 De Ville; Yᵃ 29 D'Heu de Ste Rheuse; Yᵃ 29 Le Maire. See also Mousnier, *Organes de l'État*, p. 212, and Church, *Revolution and Red Tape*, p. 40, for other examples of patronage.

Saint-Germain's regulations of 1776 envisioned that each would receive 15,000 *livres*, though they were supposed to give up sinecures. The pay scale for ordinary *commis* began at 600 *livres* and ranged to between 1,000 and 5,000; Church notes, however, that most *commis* still earned less than 2,500 *livres* at the end of their working lives. A few even entered the war bureaus without salary in order to advance their careers.[21]

Appointments did not really reflect income. Like other departments, the war office had means to reward work, especially for *premier commis*. "Gratifications," which Church compares to university merit increments or adjustments in pay irregularities, were given annually as well as in special circumstances—500 *livres* to Briquet, a *premier commis*, to help confirm his letters of nobility; 1,600 to Ségent, another *premier commis*, to help with his expenses in severe illness; and money for Allouard on the birth of his fourth child. Both *commis* and *premier commis* could expect these grants.[22]

Similarly, both could expect two types of pensions: those paid during one's career as a reward ͵or services, and those paid in retirements. For example, Charles d'Heu asked for a pension in 1737 after forty-nine years of service; he obtained one for 2,000 *livres*, and in 1740, 1741, and 1742 he also obtained gratifications of 4,000 *livres*. On his retirement in 1745 these were combined into 6,000 *livres* of pension.[23] But d'Heu did not obtain as much as Pinsonneau, a *premier commis* who had a seat on the war council of the *polysynodie*.

---

[21]Church, *Revolution and Red Tape*, p. 33; Samoyault, "Bureaux du secrétariat d'état," p. 201. See also Buot de l'Épine, "Bureaux de la guerre," p. 537. Charles D'Heu is an example of a *commis* who entered the war bureau, May 1, 1668, without pay; Y^a 29 D'Heu.

[22]Church, *Revolution and Red Tape*, p. 38; Samoyault, "Bureau du secrétariat d'état," in chap. 3 on "Traitements et pensions," pp. 179–202. In the foreign affairs office there was also a gratification for the bureaus each year that was divided among the *premier commis*. I assume the situation was similar in the war department, but this is not indicated by the Y^a 26–31 pension files. There were also annual gratifications to individuals in the foreign affairs office. Y^a 26 Briquet; Y^a 31 Ségent; Y^a 26 Allouard. See also Y^a 26 Albert.

[23]Y^a 28 D'Heu.

By a brevet in 1721, several earlier pensions were combined into one for 10,000 *livres*. These figures illustrate the variation among the *commis*. Charpentier de Jossigny, retiring in 1721, got only 6,000 *livres*. Because many *premier commis* also held the office of *commissaire des guerres* (indeed, Saint-Germain's 1776 regulations envisioned that every *premier commis* would hold that charge), their retirement incomes increased. Fumeron retired in 1771 on 12,000 *livres* of wages, plus 6,000 as military commissioner (an office he obtained in 1728), 1,800 *livres* as interpreter for an Irish-speaking regiment from County Clare, and 3,000 *livres* for past services by his family—a total of 22,800 *livres*. François de Chennevières, who retired the same year, gained a total of 18,000.[24]

Throughout the century, ordinary *commis* received much less. Michellet de Belairmont retired in 1729 at age seventy-one with just 600 *livres*. An earlier *commis*, Le Beuf, got 1,500 *livres* in 1702; Seroux, a later one, 1,200 *livres* in 1763. In 1768, Le Changeur was exceptional, with 3,000 *livres* for his retirement, including 1,200 revertible to his wife.[25]

Unfortunately, these figures do not tell us much about the financial position of *commis*. We know little or nothing about inherited wealth. Moreover, *premier commis* were often rewarded with lucrative sinecures such as offices in the order of St. Louis, in which ten *premier commis* served as treasurers, controllers, or intendants in the eighteenth century. Others acquired valuable gifts from the Crown, such as rights over vehicles at court worth 20,000 *livres* annually. Pinsonneau represented those *premier commis* who combined appointments elsewhere—he was a magistrate in the chamber of accounts and seems to have been very well-to-do. Dangeau's journal mentions that he had sold for over 1,100,000 *francs* a property in Berry that

---

[24]Y^a 30 Pinsonneau; Y^a 29 Jossigny; Y^a 28 Fumeron de Verrières; Y^a 27 Chennevières. See also Y^a 31 Ségent. For Saint-Germain's project regarding *commissaires des guerres*, see Church, *Revolution and Red Tape*, p. 33, and Buot de l'Épine, "Bureau de la guerre," p. 537.

[25]Y^a 30 Michellet de Belairmont; Y^a 29 Le Beuf; Y^a 31 Seroux; Y^a 29 Le Changeur. See also Y^a 30 Monteil.

had cost him 400,000. Common parlance had it that while the position of *premier commis* was not very spectacular, it could be very profitable.[26]

Perhaps for this reason some *premier commis* spoke of their disinterest in material gain during their years of service. Briquet told the minister in 1738 that he had worked for forty-eight years "intent on meriting the grace of His Majesty and always timid when it has been a question of asking for such. I have deferred until now to represent my services and my needs. . . . I find myself without goods; my situation, known at court and among the public, proves the disinterestedness with which I have fulfilled my functions." François de Chennevières declared that in all of his appointments as *commissaire ordonnateur* charged with army provisioning, "he had never returned richer." Indeed, for his thirty years as *premier commis*, his salary "had always been below those of his colleagues."[27]

The king was urged to give pensions and gratifications to encourage others to serve as well. As d'Heu put it, a grant to himself "would encourage as well the subordinates who shared his work." And there is no doubt that encouragement was needed for those who "passed their life in a bondage and daily travail from morning to evening without any other object of honor or of fortune. It is perhaps the sole profession in the world which is so dull" because of

---

[26]*Mémoires historiques concernant l'ordre royal et militaire de Saint-Louis et l'institution du mérite militaire* (Paris: Imprimerie royale, 1785), pp. 198–210, lists: Tourmont, Pinsonneau, Marie, Caron, Le Tourneur, Claverie de Bannière, Dubuisson, Fumeron de Verrières, Chennevières, and Mélin. Y[a] 29 Laurent notes that Madame de Fresnoy, widow of a seventeenth-century *commis*, Hélie de Fresnoy, had "la jouissance des dons du feu Roy à Madame et à son mary sur les voitures de la cour et les portes de Paris ce qui luy valloit de 20,000 # de rente." Pinsonneau was received as *maître des comptes*, June 20, 1704, and did not leave the war office until after 1718, although he remained in the *Chambre des Comptes*. See Bibliothèque Nationale, Paris, MS. français 32142, "Catalogue des présidents, conseillers et officiers de la Chambre des Comptes," fol. 128 recto. Philippe de Courcillon, Marquis de Dangeau, *Journal du marquis de Dangeau*, ed. Soulié et al. (Paris: Firmin-Didot frères, 1854–60), 18:163. On the wealth of *premier commis* see Louis François du Bouchet, Marquis de Sourches (supposed author), *Mémoires du Marquis de Sourches*, ed. Comte de Cosnac (Paris: Hachette, 1882–93), 7:66, n. 2.

[27]Y[a] 26 Briquet; Y[a] 27 Chennevières. See also Y[a] 28 Fumeron de Verrières.

the "painful and continual work"; Alexandre voiced the same theme.[28] With this in mind, the modern reader is even more sympathetic to the ordinary *commis* who did not have the fortunes of their superiors. Thibault Senior in 1724 noted that his 700 *livres* of appointments did "not permit him and his family to live." Marchand's widow voiced the same complaint, as her late husband's salary "scarcely permitted him and his family to live without being able to save the least thing."[29]

Consequently the *commis* worked until ill health or death forced them to leave the office. Fortunately, the war office had no mandatory retirement age. Pinard died at age eighty in 1749, having "worked until the last moment, having been ill from an inflammation of the lungs for only four days." When Charpentier de Jossigny asked to retire in 1723 after fifty years, he was "no longer in condition to work." Chennevières likewise retired because "he is absolutely unable to continue his functions." By 1729, when Michellet de Belairmont, "one of the oldest and most ancient *commis*," pleaded his poverty and family responsibilities, we read that his "eyesight and chest are so feeble that he cannot continue the work he has done for thirty-seven years." Poor eyesight was a common complaint leading to retirement. Pinsot in 1786 suffered from "extreme feebleness of view, he can only write with a loupe." Another *commis*, Michel Godard, went blind while working in the war department.[30]

Jean-Pierre Gutton has remarked that whenever one examines documents dealing with the poor in eighteenth-century France, one is struck by the great number of widows,[31] which is also true of military pension files. Numerous requests by widows speak of their

---

[28]Y[a] 28 D'Heu; Y[a] 26 Allouard contains Alexandre's statement.
[29]Y[a] 31 Thibault (père); Y[a] 30 Marchand.
[30]Y[a] 30 Pinard (oncle); Y[a] 29 Jossigny; Y[a] 27 Chennevières; Y[a] 30 Michellet de Belairmont; Y[a] 30 Pinsot; Y[a] 28 Godard. See also Y[a] 31 Regemont and Y[a] 31 Ratte.
[31]Jean-Pierre Gutton, *La Société et les pauvres; l'exemple de la généralité de Lyon, 1534–1789* (Paris: Les Belles Lettres, 1971), p. 36.

desperate plight. Widows, of course, were seen as the "deserving poor" of Christ to whom one owed pity and charity. Generally, widows of *premier commis* suffered less than widows of the common clerks who depended upon their husbands' income and could be reduced to pitiful circumstances when they received only a third or half of that amount in pensions. It was especially hard when there were children. Alexandre in 1740 asked for aid for a widow and four children of a *commis* whose goods were "well below the mediocre." In 1758 another *premier commis* wrote on behalf of Laurens's wife: "this poor widow is eighty years old, she is burdened by infirmities, without goods, and has no resources to live by except the goodness of Monseigneur"; he noted that it was customary to accord "these sorts of widows" a pension of 600 *livres*.[32] Some widows provided certification of their plight from parish priests or other officials.[33]

Not only the *commis*'s widow but his children and other relatives also expected to obtain financial assistance, continuing for several generations. When Alexandre's *premier commis* father died, the king accorded his widow and three adult children pensions of 500 *livres* each. Upon the death of one of the sons, his pension passed to his children. After Alexandre's death in 1742, his sister asked for her deceased brother's pension of 3,000 *livres* because she and her brother had undertaken the education of a nephew. She did not get the pension, but the nephew received 500 *livres*. In another example, Briquet's daughter, a widow, got the continuation of her deceased mother's 3,000 *livres* pension. This might be expected, for her father had been an important *premier commis;* but in 1769 her son-in-law, also *premier commis,* asked for the woman's pension, noting that he was the most senior chief in service. He also asked that after his death part of the pension be paid to a son, a sublieutenant in the dragoons, to help support him in the service.[34] Provisions for nieces

---

[32] Y[a] 26 Allouard; Y[a] 29 Laurent; Y[a]30 Millot. See also Y[a] 31 Seroux.

[33] Y[a] 30 Marchand; Y[a] 26 Agogué; Y[a] 28 Fleury.

[34] Y[a] 26 Alexandre; Y[a] 26 Briquet; Y[a] 28 Fumeron de Verrières.

were also made, based upon claims of kinship and economic dependence.[35]

In conclusion, pension records tell us about the expectations of bureaucrats in the eighteenth-century French war department, halfway between two worlds: one patrimonial, the other modern. Their requests cite precedent, merit, lack of self-interest, seniority and length of service, as well as financial need. It became customary long before the 1776 regulations for clerks to expect pensions for themselves and their families. They expected that after years of "painful and continual work" they and their wives would be able to live out their lives without concern for basic necessities. The war department, like other French government departments, accepted this principle, and the expectation of retirement pensions has been seen as one of the signs of the transformation of clerks into a modern civil service. "The retirement pension quickly emerged, with security of employment," one Frenchman suggests, "as the trump-card of the public sector in its efforts at recruitment."[36] It was that, but in this period the service still partook of a much older system, nonuniform and irregular, where petitions spoke of patrons, of family service, of fidelity to the minister and his predecessors, and of obligation in return for protection and assistance. No rules required this, only custom, that a master take care of his people—not just his clerks and their wives but their children and other relatives who saw themselves as a group, a solidarity, which merited their lord's favor because of their service.

---

[35]Yᵃ 27 Chennevières; Yᵃ 28 Gondouin; Yᵃ 28 Gambier de Campy, Nicolas-Jean; Yᵃ 30 Pinard (oncle); Yᵃ 28 Gardien.

[36]Jean Tulard, "Préface: plaidoyer pour une 'autre histoire,' " in Guy Thuillier, *Bureaucratie et Bureaucrates en France au XIXe siècle* (Geneva: Librairie Droz, 1980), p. xi.

Greene's Strategy in the Southern Campaign, 1780–1781

LAWRENCE E. BABITS

*M*any historians have studied aspects of Nathanael Greene's southern campaign, but few have sought to do more than describe the troop movements and battles. Their observations are generally limited to a tactical perspective with dim reminders of the strategic situation. A notable exception to this pattern can be found in Hugh Rankin's work, which describes the political situation and the raising of North Carolina troops.[1] This essay will explore some of the broader strategic conceptions brought to the Carolinas and Virginia by Nathanael Greene.

Since I am primarily an archaeologist trained in anthropology, my approach may seem outside the view of academic history as written documentation. Most of my information was accumulated while preparing a dissertation on the creation of the archaeological record in eighteenth-century military camps. Consequently, this essay concerns material culture as seen through documents of the period. Because Nathanael Greene had been quartermaster general of the Continental army, the use of material culture to explain his strategic concepts seems justified.

[1]Hugh Rankin, *The North Carolina Continentals* (Chapel Hill: University of North Carolina Press, 1971).

135

In the context of this essay, *strategy* will follow a wider definition than that of Karl von Clausewitz, who saw it as the combination of single engagements to obtain the object of war.[2] Here *strategy* is the "comprehensive direction of power"[3] in the sense of "preparation for and waging of war."[4] Greene's own use of strategy was far more than the "art of the general" ascribed to eighteenth-century military practice and more in keeping with twentieth-century concepts that involve a "combination of political, economic, technological, and psychological factors, along with the military elements."[5] In some respects, it might be seen as demonstrating "grand strategy."[6]

Nathanael Greene mobilized the Carolinas and Virginia to conduct a campaign that freed the southernmost colonies from British control. The mobilization not only raised manpower for his regiments but also involved the basic fabric of the countryside to obtain matériel and sustenance, nurturing a political apparatus while conducting military operations against the British. This interpretation is abstracted from a detailed study of the supply situation and movements of the southern army during 1780 and 1781. Indeed, Greene's correspondence throughout the campaign is taken up more with details of supplies than with troop movements. Numerous letters report the ill-clothed state of the men, broken-down wagons, shortages of forage and equipment. This seems more the correspondence of a quartermaster general, which Greene had been, than that of an army commander.

Greene's army was hardly a major force. He had the Maryland and Delaware Line, remnants of nine regiments consolidated into

[2]Karl von Clausewitz, *On War* (Washington, D.C.: Combat Forces, 1953).

[3]Herbert Roskinski, "New Thoughts on Strategy," in B. Mitchell Simpson, ed., *War, Strategy, and Maritime Power* (New Brunswick: Rutgers University Press, 1977), pp. 63–66.

[4]Maurice Matloff, *American Military History* (Washington, D.C.: Government Printing Office, 1969), p. 11.

[5]Ibid.

[6]Quincy Wright, *A Study of War* (Chicago: University of Chicago Press, 1942), p. 292.

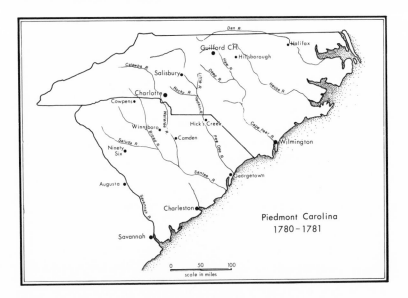

Piedmont Carolina
1780-1781

two; the cavalry of William Washington and the Partisan Legion of Henry Lee. In addition to these regular forces, he also had remnants of Buford's regiment of Virginia Continentals and a newly raised Virginia regiment. On occasion, he could call out the militia, but he constantly deprecated them. Only after the battle at Guilford Court House did North Carolina provide a partial regiment of regulars, something South Carolina never did. In both states, however, numerous irregular groups turned out, and some of them were surprisingly good. In sum, Greene's army usually consisted of less than 1,500 regulars, little more than a regiment according to the normal table of organization.

With such small numbers, most of Greene's tactical instructions were undoubtedly given orally. Historians have pieced these to-gether by examining battle situations and recollections of participants. The strategy of keeping an army in the field, supplied and fed, has largely been neglected even though Greene was more a strategist than a tactician. By examining the supply, maneuvers, and planning involving the entire capability of the Carolinas to wage war, we see that Greene was an excellent strategist in the modern meaning of the term.

The Carolinas in 1780–81 were politically organized in such a way as to be most useful to the Continental army. Political power or status was rewarded during the eighteenth century by assigning rank in militia organizations oriented along county lines.[7] The more powerful, and if possible richer, a person was, the higher his rank in the militia.[8] At the top of the structure were the county colonels. Subject to the colonels, two majors and up to twelve captains might be located within a single county.[9] Numerous junior officers and the vast body of male citizens served under them. The militia functioned politically by forcing members of a community either to turn out for duty, and thus be recognized as supporting the revolutionary movement, or to refuse and be regarded as Loyalist.[10] Greene's constant demands for troops enhanced this political function: men who refused to serve risked identifying themselves as subversive elements liable to punitive action.

The militia also functioned in a material strategic sense by serving as the collection agency for the Continental army.[11] Many details of

[7]Clarence L. Ver Steeg, *The Formative Years, 1607–1763* (New York: Hill and Wang, 1964), p. 72.

[8]John P. Shy, *A People Numerous and Armed* (New York: Oxford University Press, 1976), pp. 24, 220.

[9]Henry A. London, *An Address on the Revolutionary History of Chatham County, North Carolina* (Sanford: Cole, 1876), p. 11.

[10]Harold Carter, "Military Organization as a Response to Residence and Size of Population: a Cross-Cultural Study," *Behavior Science Research* 12 (1977): 283.

[11]Nathanael Greene to Mordecai Gist, January 23, 1781, Nathanael Greene Papers, William L. Clements Library, University of Michigan (hereafter G.P.). Lt. Colonel Mountflorence, Account of provision collected . . . , Treasurer and Comptrollers Papers, Military Papers, box 6, North Carolina Archives, Raleigh. William Smallwood to Horatio Gates, October 31, 1780, Maryland State Papers, Brown Book, item 398, Maryland Archives, Annapolis.

the supply situation can be deduced from Greene's correspondence with local colonels. The citizenry was used to extract diminishing food supplies from an area already disrupted by natural disasters as well as by two armies: a method shown particularly effective elsewhere.[12]

Greene was operating with an army that was basically infantry. This force was capable of some extended marches, but its average daily distance was approximately 12.75 miles.[13] In an extreme case, the army was capable of marching over 30 miles at a time, but this distance would require a longer resting period. In part this distance reflected the settlement pattern of the region, but other factors affecting it included poor roads and the lack of adequate transport for equipment and provisions.[14] The army usually marched from early morning to about noon, when it camped. Greene's army chose campsites close to mills virtually every night, although some of them were remote from the army.[15] Since the army spread out over one mile as it marched, headquarters and a portion of the army might be at the mill itself while other units could be quite some distance away.[16] In addition to open space, water, and grain—the normal reasons for camping at a mill—Greene chose such sites to exploit most effectively the regions through which he marched. Mills were associated with county-level structures of command, as shown by the militia ranks given to mill owners. Many of the mills were owned, if not operated, by members of the local elite.[17] Thus Greene

[12]Rankin, *North Carolina Continentals*, p. 264. Carole A. Smith, "Exchange Systems and the Spatial Distribution of Elites: The Organization of Stratification in Agrarian Societies," in Carole A. Smith, ed., *Regional Analyses* (New York: Academic, 1976), p. 330.

[13]Lawrence E. Babits, "Military Documents and Archaeological Sites: Methodological Contributions to Historical Archaeology" (Ph.d. diss., Brown University, 1981), p. 62. Joseph B. Turner, ed., *The Journal and Order Book of Captain Robert Kirkwood* (Wilmington: Historical Society of Delaware, 1910), p. 13.

[14]Mordecai Gist, Orderly Book, MS. 390, vol. 3, Maryland Historical Society. William Smallwood, Orderly Book, Domestic Collection, Library of Congress.

[15]Babits, "Military Documents," p. 88.

[16]James Mercur, *Elements of the Art of War* (London: Macmillan, 1889), p. 127.

[17]Babits, "Military Documents," p. 93.

as military commander forced the local leadership to produce the supplies that his army needed, simply by operating within the chain of command. In effect, Greene mobilized an existing political and military structure to meet short- and long-term requirements of his soldiery. This approach enhanced the stability of the patriot political system while it also identified those who did not support the cause.

It is axiomatic that an army travels on its stomach. Greene's infantrymen were no different, and their fare was lean indeed. On many occasions, they went without food; their rations rarely came close to those stipulated by regulations. Greene made tremendous efforts to procure foodstuffs for his army: one could make an illuminating study of his writings to determine the percentage of his letters that dealt with food. His strategic use of the Piedmont to feed his men is illustrated by two typical examples.

The first begins with a letter describing the gathering of supplies for the army by militia forces operating around the Moravian settlements in early 1781. Although the Moravian villages were somewhat to the north of the line of march of both the "flying army" and the main army, Greene's commissary troops were seeking supplies in advance of them. These supplies would be ground at mills near Guilford Court House.[18] Sweeping up flour speeded issuing to the Continentals, and gathering grain also interfered with the British food supply. It is a particularly succinct commentary on the supply situation and the fluid nature of the campaign that I have yet to identify a single instance of mill destruction by either side. While Greene did not specify that all materials were to be removed by foraging parties during February 1781, it is clear that this sort of operation was underway. Greene certainly ordered the total removal of supplies ahead of the British in March 1781.[19]

When Greene marched his army back to South Carolina in April, he moved slowly enough that supplies could be laid in at mills ahead

---

[18]Daniel Morgan to Nathanael Greene, February 7, 1781, Harvard University Library. Moravian complaint letter, people of Salem, N.C., to Nathanael Greene, February 8, 1781, Library of Congress.

[19]Nathanael Greene to Francis Malmedy, March 18, 1781, G.P.

of the line of march. To ensure foodstuffs on the march, he ordered the county colonels to bring grain to central locations. This procedure can be seen in letters of Colonel Thomas Wade, written from Haley's Ferry, a day's march ahead of the main army then at Kimbrough's Mill on Little River.[20] Three days later, the army was at May's Mill, where the provisions were apparently insufficient, for they stayed only one night.[21]

The importance of prepositioning supplies cannot be overestimated. It was necessary to rest the horses, if not the men, at five- to seven-day intervals.[22] An overnight stop became a two-day stay, virtually exhausting local supplies if they had not been augmented in advance.[23] Greene clearly understood this. Of the 133 camps between June 1, 1780, and August 30, 1781, only 42, or 31.5 percent lasted more than one night. Only 15 camps lasted for more than three nights, and only 18 were two or three nights long. The poor roads and transport are reflected in camp duration. Greene's planning coped with the problem by storing supplies ahead of the army on the march. He ordered Thomas Polk to maintain a three-day supply of provisions at magazines within two weeks of his arrival at Charlotte in December 1780.[24] Consequently, the army could rest at least one day and still have sustenance to march to another supply point. The army moved in accord with supplies gathered ahead of it as much as in response to enemy movements or to the supplies available at its current location.

At no time did the army issue more than three days' rations to the men during the southern campaign. The men would have had to carry the provisions, and probably they would have dealt with the added weight by consuming it immediately, especially given their

[20]Nathaniel Pendleton, Orderly Book, 1781, Library of Congress. Thomas Wade to Nathanael Greene, April 12, 1781, G.P.

[21]Nathaniel Pendleton, Orderly Book, 1781, Library of Congress.

[22]Donald W. Engels, *Alexander the Great and the Logistics of the Macedonian Army* (Berkeley and Los Angeles: University of California Press, 1978), pp. 154–55.

[23]Ibid., pp. 45–46.

[24]Nathanael Greene to Thomas Polk, December 1780, in *State Records of North Carolina* 15:179.

limited diet. Yet the requirement for three days' rations, which is
repeated on numerous occasions, has antecedents related to infantry
marching and carrying rates as far back as Alexander the Great. It
was simply impossible for infantry to carry more than three days'
rations.[25]

As a result of his experiences in the north and because of the
situation in the south, Greene became his own quartermaster general while directing the army. As he went south in October and
November 1780, Greene had called on Congress and the state
legislatures to provide the needed supplies. These were easily
promised but obtained only with great difficulty. Nevertheless, the
long-range planning instituted by Greene from the start of his
journey was to pay dividends in the early summer of 1781. The
shipment of clothing that reached Greene's army at Ninety Six
illustrates his strategic sense. The supply convoy originated in
Philadelphia, although some of the clothing may have come from
Newburgh, New York. Timothy Pickering's letter to Greene on
February 3, 1781, mentions that twenty-five wagons were heading
from Philadelphia for the southern army.[26] But the convoy did not
leave until at least March 29, the date of invoices for the supplies;
indeed, by April 5, another letter from Philadelphia reported that a
wagon train directed by Barney Hunt was underway.[27] By the end
of April, the convoy had reached Carter's Ferry, Virginia, but then
had only twenty-four wagons and was without guards.[28] When it
reached Salisbury, North Carolina, by May 17, two more wagons
had been lost in transport.[29]

[25]Engels, *Alexander the Great*, pp. 21–22.

[26]Timothy Pickering to Nathanael Greene, February 3, 1781, Library of Congress.

[27]These invoices note the quantity of material in each box and give box numbers; it
is therefore possible to trace these items fairly easily. John Macklin, "Invoice of
Goods sent to the Southern Army," G.P. George Walton to Nathanael Greene, in
The History of America in Documents, pt. 3 (Philadelphia: Rosenbach, 1949–51), p. 203.

[28]Thomas Compty to Nathanael Greene, April 28, 1781, G.P.

[29]James Read to Nathanael Greene, May 17, 1781, G.P.

On May 21, Greene sent his aide, Major Lewis Morris, to bring the convoy from Salisbury.[30] Greene was about to commence siege operations at Ninety Six, yet he appeared more concerned with outfitting his troops than preparing for the siege. Morris was at Charlotte three days later and ordered the brigade of wagons and troops from Salisbury to join the army. His directions were quite explicit, listing each stopping place and river crossing.[31] On June 1, the supplies had reached the army, because a record of clothing wanted was made at Ninety Six.[32] The clothier general for Maryland reported issuing the clothing on June 10; consequently, the uniforms reached troops in the field some seventy days after leaving Philadelphia.[33]

Anyone who studies the returns, invoices, and issuing receipts will note that the invoices contain few references to overalls, although many were issued. Overalls were obtained during the halt at Salisbury, by then a major center of shirt and overall production for Greene's army.[34] Greene had encouraged this industry in the countryside around Salisbury since December 1780, and by May 1781 his army reaped the benefits.[35] In this example, it is clear that Greene's planning involved the total resources of the area. The people had been called upon to provide supplements long before the actual need. This is not readily apparent unless we compare supply records, identifying what was brought from the north, and what was actually issued. It is certain that the southern army would have gone without overalls if Greene had lacked the foresight to order them made locally some six months before.

---

[30]Nathanael Greene to Lewis Morris, May 21, 1781, G.P.

[31]Lewis Morris to ?, May 24, 1781, G.P.

[32]"General Return of Cloathing," June 1, 1781, G.P.

[33]John Randall, "Accounts of the Clothier General for Maryland, 1780–81," Manuscript 1814, Maryland Historical Society.

[34]Nathanael Greene to Joseph Marbury, January 16, 1781, and Joseph Marbury to Ichabod Burnet, January 16, 1781, G.P.

[35]R. Smith to Nathanael Greene, July 7, 1781, G.P.

Greene's foresight can be seen in the calls he paid on state legislatures on his trip south when he requisitioned supplies and clothing.[36] This action indicates he had some knowledge of the problems of the southern army. The situation was worse than he imagined, however, and his men were probably in more dire straits in January 1781 than at any time later.

Greene was so distressed at the condition of his troops that he paraded them so that paroled officers returning north from Charleston could carry first-hand accounts of the disaster to their legislatures.[37] While accounts of poor clothing exist after January 1781, they are relatively mild compared to those Greene wrote during the camp on Hick's Creek.[38] A comparison of the army over time would probably show that the same troops under Gates suffered more to less account than when they served under Greene. The suffering in December and January was certainly Gates's fault, and Greene was successful in alleviating the problem to some extent.

Encouragement of local industry can also be seen in Greene's arms and ammunition supply, as the astute former quartermaster general started one laboratory at Salisbury, North Carolina, a second in Virginia, and a third at Salem or Bethabara, North Carolina.[39] Although they had constant problems, all of these operations continued to supply the army with matériel. The major difficulty seems to have been transport and its susceptibility to the weather—cartridges and clothing were often reported wet and damaged.[40] Munitions were also brought overland from the north. Among the twenty-two

[36]Requisition of Nathanael Greene on the State of Maryland, November 10, 1780, Maryland State Papers, item 403.

[37]Nathanael Greene to Chevalier de la Luzerne, January 9, 1781, G.P.

[38]Nathanael Greene to Abner Nash, January 7, 1781, Library of Congress; Nathanael Greene to John Cox, January 9, 1781, G.P.; Nathanael Greene to Thomas Sumter, January 15, 1781, Library of Congress.

[39]Nathanael Greene to the Board of War, July 28, 1781, and to Baron Von Steuben, March 5, 1781, G.P. Nathanael Greene to Joseph Marbury, January 7, 1781, Library of Congress.

[40]John Hamilton to Nathanael Greene, September 10, 1781, G.P. Rankin, *North Carolina Continentals*, p. 324.

wagons that finally reached Salisbury in May, ten contained ammunition. At the start of the journey these supplies included nearly 100,000 musket cartridges and assorted shot for artillery.[41] Given the amount of matériel damaged in transit, local production of ammunition was a necessity if Greene's troops were to continue the struggle. Again, the long-range planning instituted by Greene in December 1780 and January 1781 was crucial to his army's ability to fight in May, June, and July, when the British were driven into coastal South Carolina.

In response to his constant problems with transportation, Greene tried in March 1781 to convert wagon convoys to pack trains. This was an intelligent response to the crude roads and sorry state of equipment, but it never rid the army of its transport woes, because wagons continued to be used.[42]

Perhaps the most revealing aspect of Greene's strategic sense was his movement of troops around the Piedmont. The need for short stays in camps because of rapid depletion of food supplies already has been mentioned.[43] At the longer camps, Greene resorted to another method of supply. This approach drew on the river system of the Piedmont, and it is a key to understanding Greene's strategy. In conjunction with his placement of long-term camps and troop movements, Greene made a major strategic decision in December 1780. He sent Daniel Morgan and a "flying army" to the west while he moved the main force to the Pee Dee River just below the North Carolina border. His division of forces might be seen as violating the principle of mass, but Greene was utilizing economy of force to achieve a portion of his strategy—breaking "down the enemy's control while simultaneously preventing him from interfering" with the main army.[44]

At the main camp at Hick's Creek on the Pee Dee River, Greene busied his army in many ways while the militia continued to provide

[41]J. Compty, "Invoice of cannon and musket ammunition," March 29, 1781, G.P.
[42]Ichabod Burnet to Nathanael Greene, March 4, 1781, G.P.
[43]Engels, *Alexander the Great*, pp. 45–46.
[44]Roskinski, "New Thoughts," p. 64.

supplies. The transport of those supplies had changed somewhat, with calls for boatmen to bring in the foodstuffs—now Greene was using water transport in addition to wagons.[45] At the same time, boats were constructed with wheels to enable them to move with the army on land and water.[46] These activities reflect Greene's sense of the strategic value of the river system in Piedmont Carolina.

At Hick's Creek, Greene also authorized a raid on Georgetown, South Carolina, including an assault by troops floated down the Pee Dee to land at the town docks. Knowledge of the river system enabled the tactical attack to be carried out. But in a strategic sense, this little-known attack on Georgetown, to the east of the main British outposts at Camden, Winnsboro, and Ninety Six, might have shifted British attention away from Morgan's small force operating on the headwaters of the Broad River. It certainly tends to confirm the statement that Greene understood the rivers better than those who had grown up in the vicinity of the Catawba, another river he utilized in his campaign.[47]

Greene's strategy in dividing his forces thus becomes more clear. He sought better opportunities to obtain supplies while disrupting British attempts to forage in the same area. By controlling the headwaters of drainage systems from which the British derived their sustenance, Morgan, Greene, and their partisans intercepted the supplies at their source. The British did not adequately report that they were using watercraft to provide transport for supplies, but there are some references to that effect.[48] If the British were supplying their outlying garrisons by water, then those supplies had to be moved upstream, against the currents in storm-swollen rivers, after Morgan and Greene moved to their positions in December 1780, when they effectively cut all rivers above the garrisons.

[45]Nathanael Greene to James A. Lillington, January 16, 1781, G.P.

[46]Nathanael Greene to Daniel Morgan, January 19, 1781, G.P.

[47]Rankin, *North Carolina Continentals*, p. 274.

[48]R. Arthur Bowler, *Logistics and the Failure of the British Army in America* (Princeton: Princeton University Press, 1975), pp. 90–91.

Another example of strategic riverine use can be seen for the period after Morgan's defeat of Colonel Banastre Tarleton at Cowpens on January 17, 1781. Greene made a rapid withdrawal to Virginia that broke the back of the British supply system. General Charles Cornwallis even destroyed his wagon train to lighten his troops for the pursuit through areas Greene had occupied. As Greene retreated, he brought all boats to his river crossings and then removed them after the American troops had passed.[49] In addition, the militia again swept the area for food supplies ahead of the armies, thereby denying both supplies and the means of transporting them to the pursuing British.

Only when Greene crossed into Virginia and found himself downstream from Cornwallis did he turn and commence the maneuvering that led to the battle at Guilford Court House. In light of his earlier interdiction of British supplies along the waterways, Greene's turning to fight can be explained as necessary. The southern army had moved onto a river system that led to another British army, located downstream. If the Americans remained on the river, they would be caught between that army and Cornwallis upstream. As it worked out, Greene had already overextended the British. Cornwallis turned and entered Hillsborough, North Carolina, in an effort to recruit more troops and resupply those he had. During the "race to the Dan," Greene had used a defensive strategy that forced the British to pursue him, while he still retained the initiative and avoided disintegration of the army. By this means he broke the British ability to wage war.[50]

For the same reasons, Greene did not follow Cornwallis to coastal North Carolina after Guilford Court House. While it was possible to obtain supplies from upstream, the area had been so thoroughly gone over by both armies that the Americans were already fainting from the lack of food just when they commenced their pursuit.[51]

[49]Rankin, *North Carolina Continentals*, p. 273.
[50]Roskinski, "New Thoughts," p. 64.
[51]Nathanael Greene to Samuel Huntington, March 30, 1781, G.P.

Unwilling to risk another period of starvation, Greene returned to South Carolina, which had provided him with food during his stay at Hick's Creek in December and January. This choice again shows his strategic sense. He began to conduct a harassing campaign against scattered British garrisons. The weaker ones were attacked and taken, while the stronger ones were subjected to a campaign of supply interdiction that eventually caused their abandonment. Greene was using the same procedure that had proved successful in January. He had partisan raiders intercept supplies heading for the British by both wagon and boat while threatening the garrisons with military force as well.[52] The interdiction of supplies continued even after the British abandoned the Piedmont to the rebels in the summer of 1781. Greene had cut off the coastal area from the hinterland and its supplies, upon which the British depended.[53] Confined to a narrow coastal strip running from north of Charleston to south of Savannah, the British were faced with the choice of abandoning the southern states or starving to death.[54]

Throughout the southern campaign Greene acted as if he were still the quartermaster general who had brought order to the supply of the Continental army under Washington. He obtained supplies for his own troops while denying them to the enemy. It was almost as if he had put himself in the place of the British army's quartermaster's office and designed the worst possible scenario for them. He used the resources of the Piedmont in a massive effort to maintain his own forces. This exploitation of political, social, economic, and military resources gave him victory and required far more than simply maneuvering his army through a series of battles. His strategic objective was to maintain his army in the field no matter what happened. Even though he suffered from bad luck and conservative judgment on the battlefield, he was successful because his

[52]Bowler, *Logistics*, pp. 90–91.
[53]Roskinski, "New Thoughts," p. 64.
[54]Bowler, *Logistics*, pp. 86–87, 98, 153.

"comprehensive direction of power" broke the British, despite never winning any battles. In this sense, his manipulation of resources was the major strategic effort of the campaign that won the south for the Revolution. His performance, added to that of Washington in the early war years, probably did more to win the war than any other campaigns. By maintaining a military presence, Greene continually demonstrated that the Revolution was still alive in the south. The British could defeat his army but they could not destroy it. His battered Continentals served as a flickering beacon of revolution in the south during 1780 and 1781. In the end, Greene's strategy of mobilizing the entire Carolina countryside to support his Maryland, Delaware, and Virginia regulars proved the key to winning the south once and for all.

Continental Army Hospitals
and American Society,
1775–1781

RICHARD L. BLANCO

In contrast to the traditional emphasis on generals and battles, more recent military history stresses the impact of warfare on society. New topics and quantitative revisions of familiar themes add to our understanding of the War of American Independence. Even military medicine of the era—the ignorance of which had distorted our comprehension of campaigns—has been thoroughly investigated (though not for practices in the south). Yet one over-looked aspect of the Revolution is how American civilians responded to army hospitals.

Disease, far more than enemy bullets and bayonets, took a fearsome toll of American troops. Civilians feared that a "plague" emanating from a military encampment would contaminate their region. Property-conscious citizens were often antagonized when army doctors and line officers seized shelters for sick and wounded troops. Did villages voluntarily offer buildings for invalid soldiers? Did settlements patriotically or charitably contribute personnel, provisions, and equipment to army hospitals? Although information about a popular response is elusive, there is enough evidence to examine another link between the military and society, particularly in the better documented northern campaigns.

Military medicine reflected the civilian level of surgery and preventive medicine in late colonial North America. Although "pest houses" for seamen and immigrants existed, the only permanent hospital was the Pennsylvania Hospital in Philadelphia. Founded in 1752 and modeled after similar European institutions, it was originally intended for paupers and "sick strangers." Private patients were treated by practitioners of their choice. The 150-bed building had staff physicians, surgeons, and apothecaries as well as laborers—matrons, nurses, stewards, cooks, and orderlies. It had the best bathing, sanitary, and ventilating arrangements on the continent, and it also contained a museum, laboratory, apothecary shop, and facilities where apprentices studied "physick." But its relative efficiency in this prescientific era of medicine is difficult to determine. Intended to treat the sick-poor who suffered from curable and noncontagious diseases, Pennsylvania Hospital excluded terminal cases and those with infectious diseases. Even so, about 12 percent of the patients perished.[1] Thus, in the most advanced medical unit in

[1]William H. Williams, *America's First Hospital: The Pennsylvania Hospital 1745–1841* (Wayne, Pa.: Haverford House, 1975), p. 67. The basic works on military medicine during the Revolution are Stanhope Bayne-Jones, *The Evolution of Preventive Medicine in the United States Army, 1607–1939* (Washington, D.C.: Office of the Surgeon General, Department of the Army, 1968), pp. 1–58; Louis C. Duncan, *Medical Men in the American Revolution, 1775–1783* (Carlisle Barracks, Pa.: Medical Field Service School, 1931); James E. Gibson, *Dr. Bodo Otto and the Medical Background of the American Revolution* (Springfield, Ill.: Charles C. Thomas, 1937); William O. Owen, ed., *The Medical Department of the United States Army (Legislative and Administrative History)* . . . *(1776–1786)* . . . (New York: Paul B. Hoeber, 1920); and Joseph M. Toner, *The Medical Men of the Revolution with a Brief History of the Continental Army* (Philadelphia: Collins, 1876).

Philip Cash, *Medical Men at the Siege of Boston, April 1775–April 1776: Problems of the Massachusetts and Continental Armies* (Philadelphia: American Philosophical Society, 1973), is outstanding for one campaign. Richardo Torres-Reyes, *Morristown National Historical Park: 1779–1780 Encampment: A Study of Medical Services* (Washington, D.C.: Office of History and Historic Architecture, Eastern Service Center, 1971), traces developments at one camp. Howard Lewis Applegate, "Constitutions Like Iron: The Life of the American Revolutionary War Soldier in the Middle Department, 1775–1783" (Ph.D. diss., Syracuse University, 1966), is a good summary of health care. A useful guide is David L. Cowen, *A Bibliography on the History of Colonial and*

the colonies, even with strict restrictions on admissions, a large number of patients died. Army hospitals, hastily established, poorly cleaned, inadequately staffed, and woefully short of drugs, fuel, straw, linen, blankets, and surgical instruments, would have far greater mortality rates and would acquire fearful reputations. As Corporal James Fergus explained when he was ordered for treatment in Charleston: "I had seen the [army] hospitals in Philadelphia,

---

Revolutionary Medicine and Pharmacy (Madison: American Institute for the History of Pharmacy, 1976).

Although abundant data are available about campaigns in the north, little information exists in print about hospital conditions in the south. Duncan, *Medical Men*, pp. 310–58, has the best coverage. See also Wyndham Bolling Blanton, *Medicine in Virginia in the Eighteenth Century* (Richmond: Garrett and Massie, 1931); Chalmers Gaston Davidson, *Friend of the People: The Life of Peter Fayssoux of Charleston* (Columbia: South Carolina Medical Association, 1950); Gordon W. Jones, "Medicine in Virginia in Revolutionary Times," *Journal of the History of Medicine and Allied Sciences* 31 (1976): 250–70; and Joseph I. Waring, *A History of Medicine in South Carolina, 1670–1825* (Charleston: South Carolina Medical Association, 1964), pp. 82–106, 340–43. Some data on southern army doctors are in John W. Neal, "Public Services of Hugh Williamson," *Trinity College Historical Society Papers* 13 (1951): 10–14; and R. W. Gibbes, ed., *Reminiscences, Documentary History of the American Revolution*, 3 vols. (New York: D. Appleton, 1853–57), 2:248–92.

For surgery, see Malcolm C. Gilman, "Military Surgery in the American Revolution," *Journal of the Medical Society of New Jersey* 57 (1960): 492–96; Mark M. Ravitch, "Surgery in 1776," *Annals of Surgery* 186 (1977): 291–300; and Allen C. Wooden, "The Wounds and Weapons of the Revolutionary War from 1775 to 1783," *Delaware Medical Journal* 33 (1972): 59–65. For pharmacy, see David L. Cowen, *The Colonial and Revolutionary Heritage of Pharmacy in America* (Trenton: New Jersey Pharmaceutical Association; Madison: American Institute of Pharmacy, 1976); and George B. Griffenhagen, "Drug Supplies in the American Revolution," *National Museum Bulletin* 225 (1961): 110–33. For casualty rates in combat, consult Howard H. Peckham, *The Toll of Independence* (Chicago: University of Chicago Press, 1974); for details on sickness in the army, see Charles H. Lesser, *The Sinews of Independence: Monthly Strength Reports of the Continental Army* (Chicago: University of Chicago Press, 1976).

Some recent studies add little analysis or fresh information. Mary C. Gillett, *The Army Medical Department, 1775–1818* (Washington, D.C.: Center of Military History, United States Army, 1981), merely summarizes a familiar story and neglects essential source material; Erma Rish, *Supplying Washington's Army* (Washington, D.C.: Center of Military History, 1981), pp. 379–415, restates standard information; and Morris H. Saffron, *Surgeon to Washington: Dr. John Cochran (1730–1803)* (New York: Columbia University Press, 1977), is a quaint genealogical account.

Princeton, and Newark and would prefer dying in the open air of the woods rather [than] be stifled to death in a crowded hospital."[2] Yet, although the public seldom appreciated their accomplishments, the army medical men checked some contagious diseases, promulgated sanitary standards, and, occasionally, won praise for heroism on bloody battlefields and in pestilential hospital wards.

Although many ranking army doctors received their training in Philadelphia, there was no formal instruction in military medicine. Few advances in either the theory or practice of medicine in America transpired during the Age of Enlightenment. No physician pondered the cellular structure of the human body, theorized that insects were vectors of pestilence, or considered a germ theory of disease. Techniques like taking a patient's pulse or temperature, or examining his bodily fluids, were rarely performed. Subjects like chemistry, neurology, pathology, and physiology were embryonic. The level of microscopy was rudimentary, and an understanding of bacteriology was a century away. Public health functioned within narrow legislative frameworks, and few regulations were enacted to protect communities from epidemics. Fears, superstitions, and religious attitudes limited a doctor's ability to stem contagion.

Inhibited by limitations of tools for examining the body, medicine suffered other restraints also. Owing to contemporary speculative pathology, doctors were usually in ignorance about the nature of illness. Medical thought was still confined to the ancient Galenic theory about the humors of the human body. Diseases were not considered distinct entities but rather disturbances, either excess or deficiency, of the four humors—blood, phlegm, black bile, and yellow bile. To restore health, doctors prescribed bloodletting, blistering, cathartics, emetics, poultices, diuretics, fomentation, salivation, "low diet," and heavy dosage of drugs as placebos. Diagnoses of common ailments provided surface clues, but doctors were baffled by the pathogenesis of disease. Unable to comprehend

[2]Cited in John C. Dann, ed., *The Revolution Remembered: Eyewitness Accounts of the War for American Independence* (Chicago: University of Chicago Press, 1979), p. 184.

bodily changes produced by disease or treatment, physicians could not visualize what was happening to their patients. For the terrible array of maladies that plagued the colonials, doctors had remedies only for scurvy, scabies, malaria, and smallpox.

American doctors usually performed surgery but in general only on the body surface and extremities. Gifted professionals operated on harelips, performed tonsillectomies, attempted paracentesis, "cut for stone" in the gall bladder, and sometimes acted as male midwives. They performed two "capital" operations—trepanning (removing bone from the cranium) and amputation. Amputations of the limbs were so dangerous that 50 percent of them were fatal in eighteenth-century Britain.[3] The surgeon could not operate on bodily cavities inasmuch as anatomical explorations of the thorax and abdomen were decades away. He knew nothing about the nature of shock, the dangers of infection, or the indications for amputation.

The wounded in combat were dragged off by comrades, carried on canvas, sailcloth, blankets, or wooden frames, or they were hauled off in carts, sleds, wagons, carriages, or wheelbarrows. If battlefield casualties survived their evacuation procedures and exposure to the elements, hemorrhaging, and resulting trauma, then their chances of acquiring tetanus and hospital gangrene were high. Contemporary accounts of probing for musket balls or amputating shattered limbs are gruesome.[4] The surgeon could dress burns and skin injuries, but he could provide little relief to men who had been hacked, pierced, scalped, twisted, and fractured.

Instead of castigating American army doctors for their supposed incompetence, one could praise them for their diligence. Six ranking

[3]F. F. Cartwright, *The Development of Modern Surgery from 1830* (New York: T. Y. Crowell, 1967), p. 13.

[4]For examples: Colonel Edward Hand to Jasper Yeates, April 24, 1775, Edward Hand Papers, New-York Historical Society. Solomon Drowne to Salley Drowne, July 13, 1776, Solomon Drowne Papers, Rhode Island Historical Society. Entries of August 23–24, 1776, Diary of Andrew Hunter, Manuscripts Room, Princeton University Library. Entries of September 1777, Journal of Major Joseph Bloomfield, Morristown National Historical Park.

physicians had served in the French and Indian War, some 200 had acquired advanced training abroad, and nearly 400 of 3,500 practitioners had medical degrees. Many knew treatises by British army and navy doctors such as John Ranby, James Lind, Donald Monro, Richard Brocklesby, and, especially, Sir John Pringle. Pringle explained how disease during the Seven Years' War had destroyed an army. He asserted that "putrid fever" (typhus) invariably resulted from cramming ill-fed, exhausted, slovenly troops into barracks and especially into hospitals improvised in barns, stables, churches, warehouses, prisons, insane asylums, poorhouses, and schools. Pringle and Monro cited regulations for administering an army hospital, diet tables, registers for patients, and duties of personnel. In particular, they stressed the need for sufficient space, ample ventilation, and care in selecting hospital sites. They advised cleaning a hospital with smoke, soap, and gunpowder.[5] But although regimental surgeons had manuals like these to guide them, including a timely summary published by Dr. James Jones of New York in 1775, such advice was frequently overlooked in the fray of battle or the frenzy of retreat. The brief time available for treating crucial cases, the flow of casualties, the surgeon's own stamina, and the shortages of equipment presented obstacles not envisioned in the textbooks. Furthermore, although Congress enacted nebulous directives about how army hospitals should be supervised, actual details were improvised by commanders and physicians in the field.

The organization of American army hospitals began after the fighting at Lexington and Concord in April 1775, when the Massachusetts Provincial Congress acquired the Cambridge Anglican Church and numerous spacious Tory homes for recuperation centers. To ward off smallpox, isolation centers were soon established. By late spring, the Bay Colony had four general hospitals—in Cambridge, Menotomy, Roxbury, and Watertown. Patriotic enthusiasm after the slaughter on Bunker Hill (June 17) was high, and

[5]See Richard L. Blanco, *Wellington's Surgeon General: Sir James McGrigor* (Durham, N.C.: Duke University Press, 1974).

numerous Bostonians offered their homes for the sick and wounded. As more volunteers arrived for the siege of Boston, Congress enacted the Hospital Bill, which established the continental medical department.[6] Barely deviating from the British model, the delegates appointed a director-general to supervise a professional staff, acquire ward attendants, organize hospitals, and perform commissary duties. Congress required that regimental hospitals under a surgeon and his mate remain close to the battlefields, while field hospitals, termed "flying" or "marching" hospitals and usually under a physician's care, would be located near combat sectors to handle casualty overflows. Finally, general hospitals were to be located safe from enemy bombardment. But the visionary theory of hospital administration lapsed into arrangements quite different from what Dr. John Morgan, the energetic second director-general had contemplated.[7] Army hospitals suffered from professional bickering, shortages of drugs and instruments, complaints about pay and status, confusion about supervising regimental surgeons, and the understandable pleas of sick soldiers to be treated by "hometown" surgeons instead of strange doctors.

Shortages of fuel, shelter, and foodstuffs affected some regiments during the siege of Boston. The main illnesses were jaundice, diarrhea, dysentery, and arthritis; respiratory ailments and contagious diseases were not widespread. Soldiers infected with smallpox were quickly quarantined. With General George Washington's support, Morgan had the entire army inoculated by March 1776. It is noteworthy that regiments composed of hastily raised units from diverse areas and crowded together under generally unsanitary conditions did not have higher rates of disease. The incidence of

[6]Cash, *Medical Men*, pp. 67–80.

[7]See the Orderly Book of Artemus Ward at the Siege of Boston, Massachusetts Historical Society; Orderly Book of Philip Schuyler, Henry E. Huntington Library (microfilm); Order Book of Horatio Gates, New-York Historical Society; General Orders by General William Moultrie and General Robert Howe, 1778, South Carolina Historical Society; Dr. Peter Fayssoux to General Benjamin Lincoln, December 1778, Benjamin Lincoln Papers, Massachusetts Historical Society; and Orders for the Establishment of a General Hospital in Rhode Island, Drowne Papers.

sickness from the nine months' siege averaged 12 percent, typical of a European campaign in that century.[8] The medical department functioned well; in fact rarely again did it perform so effectively.

Perhaps because combat was limited and the soldiers were healthy, they did not succumb more frequently. With some shameful exceptions, the troops were well sheltered, and the public was generally sympathetic to the patriot cause. When Morgan requested bandages, blankets, and leather webbing, he received an enthusiastic response. Even drugs, seized from Tory apothecary shops or from privateers that docked with prizes, were plentiful. Surgical instruments, however, remained difficult to obtain. Furthermore, many local doctors donated their services, New England governors were successful in provisioning their troops, and the campaign was conducted along static lines near populated supply and manufacturing centers. A major factor was Washington's personal interest in camp hygiene, demonstrated throughout the war in general orders testifying to his concern for the troops. One should also stress the patriotic ardor of the surrounding countryside, the availability of shelters for convalescents, and the defensive position of the redcoats with their backs to the sea. Later in the war, the cooperation between public and army was seldom as successful.

The real test of the army hospitals came during the invasion of Canada in 1775–76. Intent on making the province into the "Fourteenth Colony," Congress sent forces under Colonel Benedict Arnold through the Maine wilderness and under General Richard Montgomery through upper New York to the St. Lawrence River. Concentrating on Boston, and assuming easy victory at Quebec, the delegates failed to provide adequate hospital facilities for the northern army. In December 1775, the medical staff was preparing hospitals from Albany to Quebec when smallpox struck. Lacking the quarantine policy devised at Boston, one-third of the troops were stricken by early April. By early May, only 3,000 of 7,000 Yankees were fit for duty. Driven back by the troops of General John

[8]John Hennen, *Military Surgery* (London: A. Constable, 1820), p. 30.

Burgoyne, the American force retreated up the St. Lawrence, up the
Richelieu River, and over Lake Champlain, finding temporary
sanctuary at Fort Ticonderoga. The most disastrous American
campaign in the north ended with the loss of 5,000 men killed,
captured, or incapacitated—40 percent of the command.[9] Smallpox,
the "King of Terrors," and dysentery had destroyed an army. While
General Horatio Gates prepared to defend Ticonderoga, the sick
were boated further south to Fort George, a mere outpost for 300
men. By October, more than 3,000 soldiers were treated there at the
largest American military hospital of the war.[10]

How did civilians react to the spreading pestilence? First, Gates
ordered that women attached to Pennsylvania regiments work at
Fort George as nurses. Dr. Jonathan Potts, the deputy director-general, sent subordinates searching for drugs in upper New York and
Hampshire Grants. Because medical supplies at Manhattan and
Philadelphia were beyond reach, Potts pleaded with the inhabitants
of Albany and Salisbury for help, requesting herbals and shirts,
sheets, and aprons for bandages.[11] Salisbury sent linens, and the
committee of safety in Albany told Potts that supplies were forth-
coming.

More impressive was the joint military-civilian supervision of
inoculation of troops marching from New England to reinforce the
Lake Champlain garrisons. As dispirited veterans of the Canadian
adventure returned homeward, it was inevitable that horror stories
would spread through communities. In Massachusetts, Dr. Cotton
Tufts warned John Adams that "smallpox . . . has much retarded
the raising of recruits." Governor Jonathan Trumbull of Connecticut informed George Washington that "fear of the infection operates
strongly to prevent soldiers from entering the service [for] . . .

---

[9]Peter Force, *American Archives*, 9 vols. (Washington, D.C.: M. St. Clair Clarke and
Peter Force, 1848–53), 5th ser., 1, p. 607; and Charles Henry Jones, *The Campaign for
the Conquest of Canada* (Philadelphia: Porter and Coates, 1882), p. 97.

[10]Hospital Return, October 1776, Miscellaneous Bound Manuscripts, Massachusetts Historical Society.

[11]MS. 1967, Fort Ticonderoga Museum (hereafter cited as FTM).

scarcely one in twenty of our people has had this distemper."
Nevertheless, some brave New Englanders hurried northward along
the Connecticut River and over the Green Mountains to Lake
Champlain. On July 12, General Philip Schuyler, commander of the
northern army, advised Washington that uninoculated men "will
rather weaken than strengthen our army." From Ticonderoga,
Gates explained on August 7 that fear of smallpox caused desertions
and that unless reinforcements were halted at Skenesboro (White-
hall, New York) for inoculation and inspection, "it would be heap-
ing a hospital upon another."[12]

The generals and physicians considered how to control the situation by inoculating newcomers, by segregating them at campsites,
by forbidding self-inoculation, and by requiring men to present
certificates attesting to "official" inoculation. The citizenry invariably voiced alarms. In Williamstown, Massachusetts, terrified inhabitants protested to Gates on August 8 that Rhode Island
carpenters had inoculated themselves. To prevent contagion at
Skenesboro, where Arnold's ramshackle fleet was being constructed,
Schuyler ordered "three or four trusty officers" to guard routes to
the port. General David Waterbury, the local commander, insisted
that civilian shipwrights undergoing inoculation avoid his post until
cured. "We have got it out of this place and out of Ticonderoga, and
we are determined to use every precaution to keep it clean."[13]

Although the attempted supervision was not entirely successful, it
was a remarkable example of military-civilian cooperation. Consid-
ering the shortage of medical personnel, the number of routes to be
policed, and the vast area to be administered, this mass treatment
was generally effective. By August 28 Gates could report from

[12]L. H. Butterfield, ed., *The Diary and Autobiography of John Adams*, 4 vols. (Cam-
bridge: Harvard University Press, 1961–66), 2:61–62; Papers of the Continental
Congress, item 155, roll 166, vol. 2, fols. 205–07 (microfilm; hereafter cited as PCC);
Force, *American Archives*, 4th ser., 6, p. 820; and PCC, item 191, roll 190, fols. 13–14.

[13]Box 4, reel 2, Horatio Gates Papers, New-York Historical Society; August 17, reel
29, Philip Schuyler Papers, New York Public Library. For a summary, see James E.
Gibson, "The Role of Disease in the 70,000 Casualties in the American Revolutionary
War," *Transactions and Studies of the College of Physicians of Philadelphia* 17 (1941):121–27.

Ticonderoga that "smallpox is now totally removed from the
army."[14] Owing to General Guy Carleton's delay in attacking, to the
valiant American naval action off Valcour Island in October, and to
the lateness of the campaign season, the British withdrew to winter
quarters. The medical men, with civilian help, had played a vital
role in checking disease that could have impaired the defense of the
"Gibraltar of the North."

Meanwhile, at New York City, Washington's army readied to
defend Manhattan from a British invasion in August. With the
support of the state's convention, Morgan and his staff diligently
prepared for the fighting. The "medics" established general hospitals
at King's College, City Hospital, City Barracks, the Exchange, the
Workhouse, and (again) at numerous vacated Loyalist homes in the
Bowery. The only recorded protests by New Yorkers over the
military use of public and private buildings appear in Tory memoirs. But the public was antagonized by environmental problems
that resulted from the transformation of a commercial town into a
major military base. The city had health regulations, a garbage
collection system, and fresh pump-water that flowed from clear
ponds and bubbling brooks. But as troops poured in, the city
sanitary services collapsed, and the water supply became contami-
nated because of soldiers' unhygienic practices.[15] Dysentery, scabies, typhus, and venereal disease further ravaged the troops already
weakened by weeks of building fortifications during a torrid summer. By early October, 8,000 of 20,000 troops were sick.[16] The
disastrous battles of Long Island, Manhattan, and White Plains are
beyond the scope of this essay, but disease clearly contributed to the
plummeting morale of American troops even before the Royal Navy
appeared on the horizon.

Washington's army scattered in retreat, some to Connecticut,
some to the Hudson Highlands, and the rest to New Jersey. As

[14]Force, *American Archives*, 5th ser., 1, p. 1146.
[15]Morris H. Saffron, "Rebels and Disease: The New York Campaign of 1776,"
Academy of Medicine of New Jersey Bulletin 13 (1967): 107–18.
[16]Lesser, *Sinews of Independence*, p. xxxi.

Continental regiments disintegrated, Morgan's medical organization collapsed also. Members of his staff had deserted their patients before the relentless enemy advance. Some regiments were left without surgeons; some men bled to death without treatment. To escape, militiamen seized vehicles intended for casualties. In mid-September, Morgan moved patients from Manhattan to Hoboken and Weehawken. When the British captured Forts Lee and Washington in late November, Morgan had to evacuate his charges again to Newark and Hackensack. The stream of sick and wounded continued, and Morgan finally dispersed his patients to Amboy, Brunswick, Trenton, and Morristown in New Jersey; to Fishkill and Peekskill on the Hudson, and to Norwich and Stamford, Connecticut.[17]

Although it is difficult to generalize about the public response to thousands of helpless men transported in open carts during the winter, there are some clues. In Connecticut, village selectmen cooperated in establishing convalescent centers for 400 men. How many buildings were donated or seized in the emergency is unknown. In Newark, however, village fathers protested bitterly that Morgan used private homes as field hospitals, and other New Jersey communities objected to the presence of sick soldiers. Surgeon James Tilton commented that the troops "fell like rotten sheep as they struggled home, where they communicated the camp disease [typhus] to their neighbors, of which many died."[18] When Morgan's organization collapsed, many line officers sought their own accommodations. General James Potter of Pennsylvania housed 200 shivering militiamen in cold barns.[19] Colonel William Smallwood notified the Annapolis Council of Safety that he had withdrawn his

---

[17]See *John Morgan, Vindication of His Public Character in the Station of Director-General of the Military Hospitals, and Physician in Chief to the American Army, Anno 1776* (Boston: Powars and Willis, 1777); and Whitfield Bell, Jr., *John Morgan, Continental Doctor* (Philadelphia: University of Pennysylvania Press, 1965), pp. 187–205.

[18]James Tilton, *Economical Observations on Military Hospitals* (Wilmington, Del.: J. Wilson, 1813), p. 63.

[19]*Pennsylvania Archives*, 59 vols. (Philadelphia and Harrisburg: J. Stevens, 1852–1906), 1st ser., 5, pp. 78–79.

casualties from Morgan's jurisdiction and "placed them in comfortable houses in the country."[20] As New Jersey was abandoned to the enemy, Morgan inevitably was denounced by generals, politicians, and doctors. Even before he was curtly dismissed in January 1777, Congress ordered Dr. William Shippen, Jr., the next director-general, to prepare hospitals in Pennsylvania.

Wagonloads of sick reached Philadelphia by early December. Heretofore, Pennsylvania had been involved only peripherally in army medical affairs as civilian doctors inspected battalions, patriotic ladies contributed rags for "bandages and lint," and the council of safety prepared hospitals in the city jail and poorhouse. But in the crisis, Washington appealed to the doctors of Philadelphia. Acting promptly, the council of safety acquired fuel, straw, and provisions; it devised facilities at the Pennsylvania Hospital, the Bettering House, a smallpox hospital on Pine Street, and thirty Loyalist shops and homes. The number of invalids sheltered during the winter of 1776–77 was about 500 in December and 1,000 in January. Typhus killed innumerable soldiers, and the city was unable to handle hordes of emaciated, vermin-ridden men. John Adams mentioned that by early 1777 over 2,000 troops were buried in Potter's Field. Other locations were needed. The army requisitioned buildings in four villages, where 300 patients were housed. Another 700 were sheltered in Bethlehem, which became the second largest convalescent center in the state. Although the Moravians there under the leadership of Bishop John Ettwein were neutral, their pleas were ignored. Needing a haven with ample buildings, Congress on December 6 sent wagonloads of sick to the Single Brethren's House, which became, Ettwein stated, "a sewer of impurities." Bethlehem is important as the first religious commune to be seized as an army hospital; its mortality rate was 25 percent by March 1777.[21] In

---

[20]Force, *American Archives*, 5th ser., 2, pp. 1099–1100.

[21]For a summary of conditions, see Richard L. Blanco, "American Army Hospitals in Pennsylvania During the Revolutionary War," *Pennsylvania History* 48 (1981): 351–54.

Pennsylvania as elsewhere, public response to the presence of sick troops varied.

The campaigns of 1777 in Pennsylvania and New York were significant in both military and medical history. In preventive medicine, the mass inoculation of troops continued. From February to May, Dr. Shippen supervised the procedures of inoculation, special diet, drug dosages, and cleaning of uniforms at Germantown and at Province and Fort islands in the Delaware River. Assuring Washington about the precautions, Shippen advised that isolated troops were guarded, "and no patient is suffered to remain a minute in the City [Philadelphia] with the smallpox."[22] Similar efforts occurred at mobilization centers from Massachusetts to Virginia.

Some communities showed traditional fear of contagion. The village fathers of Watertown, Massachusetts, refused to permit soldiers to be inoculated within their jurisdiction. As John Avery, deputy secretary of state, declared: "There is an act in the Colony which prohibits inoculation except in the Town of Boston."[23] So intense was the uproar in Chester Town, Maryland, that Colonel William Richardson notified Annapolis: "I have dropped all thought of having it done here; but Doctor [Upton Scott] tells me he has a large commodious house about four miles out of town [which would be suitable]."[24] At Hanover, New Hampshire, twenty-two indignant townsmen petitioned Washington against the use of their village for inoculation. They asserted that few local families had been exposed to smallpox and that the town was already exhausted "by armies passing and repassing [leaving their sick behind] . . ."; fuel, grain, and fowl were in short supply, and "many families are left with only a woman and a number of small children."[25]

[22]Shippen to Washington, January 31, 1777, reel 36, George Washington Papers, Library of Congress (microfilm, hereafter cited as GW).

[23]Avery to General Artemus Ward, March 4, 1777, Artemus Ward Papers, Massachusetts Historical Society.

[24]Richardson to the Council of Safety, March 20, 1777, MS. 4579–81, Maryland Historical Records, Hall of Records, Annapolis.

[25]Petition of Citizens of Hanover . . . , February 12, 1777, reel 40, GW.

Regardless of such protests and others in Virginia, North Carolina, and South Carolina throughout the war, the mass inoculation of the army continued and was effective. Although the death rate caused by natural contagion averaged 16 percent for the seaboard population, the mortality rate for Continentals who underwent supervised inoculation that year was under 1 percent.[26] Mass inoculation eliminated a major obstacle to recruiting, and fresh regiments converged on the Delaware.

The relationship between army hospitals and civilians in sparsely populated upper New York and western New England in 1777 is more difficult to ascertain. As Burgoyne's British-Hessian force pressed southward, capturing Ticonderoga, Fort George, Skenesboro, and Fort Anne, the American cause seemed doomed. What saved the American army under Schuyler and Gates were Burgoyne's strategic and logistical blunders during his advance to the Hudson.

Dr. Potts, who supervised medical affairs at Saratoga, had difficulty procuring wagons for his sick in Tory Albany. We also have a glimpse of the trouble Surgeon Francis Hagen had at Bennington, Vermont, in obtaining a church meetinghouse for his patients: "The inhabitants cannot or will not furnish me with any furniture, and it seems impossible to find houses for [the wounded]."[27]

There was popular assistance to the American cause at Bemis Heights and Freeman's Farm in the form of "camp followers." These women were rarely prostitutes; usually they were wives, common-law wives, soldiers' relatives, and females who sought employment. Eighteenth-century European forces were usually accompanied by women who cooked, cleaned, mended, and nursed. The orderly books barely cite the number of women and children permitted on a march or at an encampment, but British army regulations allowed about 9 percent of a regiment's strength to be

[26]Hugh Thursfield, "Smallpox in the American War of Independence," *Annals of Medical History*, 3d ser., 4 (1942): 316.
[27]Hagen to Potts, fol. 287, Jonathan Potts Papers, Historical Society of Pennsylvania.

women and children.[28] Camp followers at the siege of Boston were forbidden by a stern Washington—to discourage venereal disease and the concealment of strong drink. But at Saratoga and elsewhere women were in combat zones. Their presence probably improved the level of sanitation and cooking and undoubtedly heightened morale.

After Burgoyne's surrender, the American medical team was inundated with casualties. How the doctors were able to transport the severely wounded by boat and wagon is not well documented. James Thacher remembered toiling in Albany with thirty other surgeons, American, British, and German, in a large building that held 550 patients.[29] When 500 more casualties arrived, Potts, a "Fighting Quaker" who may have had moral scruples about seizing shelters, requested the townsmen there and in Schenectady to provide additional space. Albany granted him a church, the spacious home of Abraham Cayler (a notorious Tory), and several "untenanted homes," a euphemism for vacated Loyalist residences; the village of Schenectady sheltered about 90 wounded.[30]

The battle of Saratoga is significant in the history of military medicine because of the praise that medical men received, in contrast to contemporary complaints about their laziness, incompetence, or inhumanity. "Rogues and thieves" was a common phrase; Washington once termed the regimental surgeons "great rascals."

[28]I have not found the exact percentage in documentation. References to the practice are mentioned by Robert Adair, Inspector of Regimental Infirmaries, in WO 1/683, fols. 313–53, and by Sir Jeremiah Fitzpatrick, Inspector of Health for Land Forces, WO 1/896, fols. 11–12, Public Record Office (hereafter cited as PRO). For a discussion of women who served as nurses attached to regiments, see Paul E. Kopperman, "Medical Services in the British Army, 1743–1783," *Journal of the History of Medicine and Allied Sciences* 34 (1979): 443–46; and Sylvia R. Frey, *The British Soldier in America: A Social History of Military Life in the Revolutionary Period* (Austin: University of Texas Press, 1981), pp. 20, 57–63.

[29]James Thacher, *A Military Journal During the American Revolutionary War From 1775–1783* (Boston: Cotton and Barnard, 1827), pp. 113–15.

[30]James E. Sullivan, ed., *Minutes of the Albany Committee of Correspondence, 1775–1778, and Minutes of the Schenectady Committee, 1775–1778*, 2 vols. (Albany: University of the State of New York, 1923–25), 1:186, 823; Potts Papers, fols. 372, 384.

But delighted with the low sickness and casualty rates, Gates made a significant effort to change this attitude. He requested that Congress award "some honorary mark of favor" to the medical staff.[31] On November 6, Congress formally lauded the army doctors for their achievements at Saratoga, the only such testimonial to the medical profession during the war.[32]

Although victorious on the Hudson in 1777, the Americans were defeated that year on the Delaware. Medical preparations for Brandywine were deplorable, and Dr. Shippen was inept. Again the system of hospitals broke down. One Maryland officer described how American wounded were summarily dumped at a Quaker meetinghouse near the battlefield. Five hundred casualties were moved to nearby towns and settlements. "The church at Reading," remarked the Reverend Henry Muhlenberg, patriarch of Lutheranism in America, "has been turned into a hospital and is filled with wounded," while other casualties were quartered "in houses here and there." Again the Pennsylvania Hospital and Bettering House in Philadelphia were used along with sites in Trenton and Princeton in New Jersey. But after a series of defeats—the British march on Philadelphia, General William Howe's victory at Germantown, and American losses of the Delaware fortresses in November—Dr. Shippen moved his casualties. Few preparations had been made for their reception. While the British held the large buildings of Philadelphia, the Continentals were severed from the Delaware; and there were few areas in the hinterlands where incapacitated men could be quartered.[33]

Thus, although Shippen apologized to Bishop Ettwein on September 18, the army again occupied Bethlehem. By early October, the three-storied Brethren's House, which had a capacity of 380 patients at four feet of space per man, was packed full. "It seemed

[31]MS. 2103, FTM.

[32]Worthington C. Ford, ed., *Journals of the Continental Congress, 1774–1789*, 34 vols. (Washington, D.C.: Government Printing Office, 1904–37), 9:870–71.

[33]Blanco, "American Army Hospitals," pp. 355–57.

[as] if the world would engulf us," wailed Ettwein, as additional wounded were placed in nearby tents and barns. The Moravians' neatly tended agricultural plots and fences were wrecked and their herds of livestock slaughtered for a hungry soldiery.[34] Just as the army was about to seize the Widow's House and the Single Sister's House, Congress intervened. As Henry Laurens of South Carolina wrote on September 22, "We desire that all Continental officers refrain from disturbing the persons or property of the Moravian Brethren, and particularly that they do not disturb or molest the Houses where the women are assembled."[35] By December, the hamlet with a normal population of 300 had more than 700 soldiers.

In October, the army established convalescent centers at eight other Pennsylvania settlements. Lititz, another Moravian commune, was occupied on December 19, as was Ephrata, belonging to the Seventh Day Baptists, on December 24. In the frenzy to house the sick, any accommodation sufficed. Barns were spacious and well ventilated, but they were damp and dirty. Churches had pews for beds but were cold and cramped. Taverns, schoolhouses, and a shoe factory were used. At Reading, 69 soldiers found sanctuary in the courthouse, Trinity Church, Reformed Church, Friends' Meeting House, the Potter's Shop, and various residences. At Lancaster, Captain Charles Lloyd and 500 troops spent six miserable weeks on cold floors without straw or blankets. Lititz, with a casualty rate of 45 percent, was another horror. At Ephrata, Hans Baer, the village miller, lamented that his parents perished from "camp fever" transmitted by the unwelcome troops and that "the disorder raged through the neighborhood and proved fatal to a great number of all ages."[36] The prevalence of disease—typhus, dysentery, and chronic respiratory ailments—undoubtedly contributed to the demoraliza-

[34]Ettwein to Shippen, December 1977, Papers of John Ettwein, Moravian Archives, Bethlehem (microfilm copy at the State Historical Society of Wisconsin).

[35]Cited by Kenneth G. Hamilton, *John Ettwein and the Moravian Church* (Bethlehem, Pa.: Times, 1940), pp. 174–75.

[36]See Blanco, "American Army Hospitals," pp. 357–58.

tion of the army and the public. When Washington's army trudged off to Valley Forge in late December, 32 percent of his men, sick present and sick absent, were listed as unfit for duty.[37]

More hospitals were created in January 1778 at Red Lion, Uwchlan, French Creek, and Yellow Springs. Muhlenberg was indignant because officers not only seized the Lutheran and Reformed churches in Lionville but "they even filled the parsonages, and afflicted [the ministers] with all kinds of persecution because [they] publicly refused to pray for Congress."[38] At the Quaker Meeting House in Uwchlan when physicians demanded the key, "the Friend who had care of the house refusing to deliver it, forcible entry was made into the house and stable."[39] Such incidents may account for Washington's request on January 5, 1778, for the construction of a permanent building at Yellow Springs, near Valley Forge. Completed in August 1778, this spacious army hospital was the only one built by congressional order during the revolutionary war.

Another interesting incident was reported by Surgeon Barnabas Binney who supervised a hospital at Pluckemin, New Jersey, which he found "utterly unfit for the reception of sick men." Consequently, in June 1778, he moved his 500 sick to "eight or ten large barns" at Readytown, near Somerset Court House. In May 1779 he needed more room because "the two churches and court houses [were] crowded to a degree dangerous to the health of the invalids."[40] Binney applied to the magistrates for space "to accommodate the convalescents. In answer, they threatened to imprison the first who shall [seize] a barn for the sake of sick soldiers." Binney's question to

[37]Lesser, *Sinews of Independence*, p. xxxi.
[38]Henry Melchior Muhlenberg, *Journals*, 3 vols., trans. Theodore G. Tappert and John W. Doberstein (Philadelphia: Muhlenberg, 1945), 2:93.
[39]Gibson, *Dr. Bodo Otto*, p. 153.
[40]Binney to Colonel Moore Furman, Somerset Court House, June 5, 1779, Letters of Barnabas Binney, Manuscripts Room, Princeton University Library.

Quartermaster General Nathanael Greene, "What's to be done?" apparently went unanswered.[41]

As farmers in New Jersey defended their property, the faculty of the College of William and Mary likewise maintained their privileges. When General Charles Lee inspected Virginia garrisons in early 1776, he requested that buildings in Williamsburg be used for sick troops. The Convention of Delegates appointed Dr. William Rickman, director-general of Virginia, and a committee to investigate. Dr. Rickman reported that the campus buildings were improperly ventilated and unsuitable: "The college has at very considerable expense been lately repaired, white-washed, and thoroughly cleaned for the reception of scholars who are expected to restore themselves to their studies." The library and laboratory might be "totally ruined" by troops. A similar response came from John Page, vice-president of the committee of safety: "as the college is the only place in the country where our youth can be tolerably educated it seems highly improper to debar ourselves from that invaluable advantage, and indeed it is the freehold of the President and Professors, we fear it will look like a violation of private property and induce an apprehension of military encroachment thereon." Fearing the wreckage of his alma mater, Page joined Dr. Rickman in recommending that the army appropriate the Governor's Palace, several nearby houses, and the "madhouse."[42]

But to place the incident in perspective, one should note that in 1777 Virginia built the Vineyard Hospital outside of Williamsburg, the only state-constructed army hospital. Likewise, when the Tidewater was ravaged by British raids in 1781, Governor Thomas

[41]Cited by Saffron, "Medical Aspects of the Middlebrook Encampments," *Journal of the Medical Society of New Jersey* 76 (1979): 376–80. There is additional information about this incident in Binney to Greene, May 18 and 19, 1779, vol. 5, fols. 39 and 44, Correspondence of Nathanael Greene, American Philosophical Society. I have not found Greene's response in the Nathanael Greene Papers held at the Library of Congress, Duke University, or at the William L. Clements Library.

[42]William T. Van Schreevan et al., *Revolutionary Virginia*, 6 vols. (Charlottesville: University Press of Virginia, 1973–), 6:279–80, 431, 509, 511.

Jefferson, another William and Mary graduate, responded with a
tough approach to Dr. Matthew Pope's request for sheltering his
sick: "Necessity is law, in time of war especially. You must therefore
take possession of any church or vacant house or houses, convenient
for the establishment of a hospital for which this shall be your
Warrant."[43] And finally, Virginia authorities did permit Rochambeau's army to use the College of William and Mary for a French
hospital in September 1781. But again, as he had done with Bishop
Ettwein, Washington apologized profusely to the college faculty.[44]

Rhode Island appeared uncooperative with the American military
as the French fleet neared the coast in June 1780. Washington
ordered Dr. James Craik to Providence to prepare for the anticipated
arrival of 1,200 to 1,500 ill French seamen and soldiers. The
commander in chief desired spacious quarters for the allies as well as
the cooperation of Governor William Greene, the state legislature,
and Rochambeau's liaison officers. But when Dr. Craik requested
the use of the College of Rhode Island [Brown University], which
had room for 600 men and only one classroom in session, he
encountered unexpected opposition. He told Washington June 7 and
10 that while the governor and council were agreeable, "many
excuses were made while [sic] I should not have it . . . Some said [the
proposed hospital] would bring Contagious Disease into the Towns,
others said it would stop the Education of youth." Others asserted
that American soldiers already had damaged the buildings and that
they feared the flight of future scholars. Consequently, Dr. Craik
had to hunt for barns and barracks fifteen to thirty miles away.
Indignant with the Yankee response, and finding only "the most
[dirty vile?] huts I ever saw and only for 150 sick," the Virginian
ironically explained that the citizenry all wanted to assist, "Yet when

[43]Jefferson to Pope, May 21, 1781, Charlottesville, Executive Letter Book, vol. 2,
Virginia State Library. There was a similar "Warrant for the Improvement of
Medicines and Chirurgical Instruments." See Board of War to Dr. William Brown,
October 14, 1780, box 1, Board of War, Revolutionary War Records, North Carolina
State Archives.

[44]See the letter of October 27, 1781, reel 81, GW. Washington's apology to Ettwein
is dated March 25, 1778, reel 48, ibid.

I point out to them the proper place or [desire] them to do it, some selfish view or other gets the better of their Public Spirit."[45]

On June 21, Dr. Craik reported that just as "both Houses" had voted to provide Rochambeau with the campus, Parson James Manning "had the great power to inflame the people and to make them believe that a Disease no less mortal than the Plague was to be brought in by the Fleet." Hence Dr. Craik was left with rotting stables for only 300 Frenchmen.[46] Another complaint was written to Washington by Commissary General Louis Dominique Ethis de Corney, who supervised preparations for the French arrival. Corney was astounded at the minister's assertions, at the repeated threats of the prominent Brown family "to blow up the Hospital," and the opprobrium and legal threats townsmen heaped on laborers renovating the college. "This Strange Conduct," Corney wrote to Washington, "is totally opposed to the sentiments that unite the two Nations."[47] However, the matter was settled; it is clear from Washington's correspondence in late June that "the Assembly have resolved to appropriate the college for the accommodation of the French sick."[48]

The battle at Guilford Court House (March 15, 1781) provides an appropriate conclusion to this survey of public responses. In the bloody contest between Nathanael Greene and Charles Cornwallis, the circumstances were unique—the bleak environment of the Carolina back country, the shortages of medical supplies and personnel for both sides, the complete collapse of Greene's hospital organization, the number of casualties, and the presence of Quakers. The mauling fight between 4,400 Americans and 2,000 British and Hessians was nearly a stalemate. With 1,900 casualties and 800 desertions, Greene withdrew to Troublesome Creek. Cornwallis held the field but with nearly one-third of his war machine shat-

---

[45]Craik to Washington, June 7 and 10, 1780, Providence, reel 67, GW.
[46]Craik to Washington, June 21, 1780, ibid.
[47]John C. Fitzpatrick, ed., *The Writings of George Washington, 1745–1799* (Washington, D.C.: Government Printing Office, 1931–44), 19:95.
[48]Ibid., p. 93.

tered—about 600 killed, wounded, or missing. The armies were too exhausted to renew combat, and both sides spent a dreary, rainy night tending their wounded, burying their dead, and searching for casualties strewn over six miles. As Washington had done with Howe, and Gates with Burgoyne, Greene and Cornwallis exchanged courteous notes amid the carnage, permitting each other to send surgeons to find their own dead. The British rested for two days and loaded their "walking wounded" into wagons. Cornwallis then began his long trek to Deep River, Cross Creek, Wilmington, and Yorktown. Fearing entrapment, and unable to transport the severely wounded, Cornwallis left about 150 prisoners and British casualties at Guilford Court House and a like number at nearby New Garden Meeting House.[49]

How many Quakers voluntarily assisted in this crisis is uncertain. The Friends donated rags and linen to both armies, searched the woods for stricken soldiers, and hauled them homeward regardless of their allegiances. There was no outcry about contagion, no defense of property rights, and no appropriation of residences by the military. Instead, Guilford Court House was a remarkable demonstration of how a community that had already suffered the depredations of American troops for months responded to the emergency.

Referring to his own Quaker heritage, and his awareness of the peace testimony, Greene wrote on March 26: "I address myself to your humanity for the sake of the suffering and wounded at Guilford Court House. As a people, I am persuaded you disclaim any connection with . . . military operations, but I know of no order of men more remarkable for . . . benevolence; and perhaps no instance ever had a higher claim on you than the unfortunate wounded in your neighborhood."[50] Four days later, the Quakers responded from New Garden:

[49]Cornwallis summarized his situation in PRO 30/11/90, fols. 187–88, and 30/11/5, fols. 117–28 (microfilm, University of Michigan Graduate Library). Greene's comments and hospital returns are in vol. 24, March 11–22, and vol. 27, Dr. William Brown to Greene, April 2, Guilford, Greene Papers, Clements Library.

[50]Cited in Russell Phillips, *North Carolina in the Revolutionary War* (Charlotte: Heritage, 1976), pp. 222–23.

Friend Greene . . . Agreeable to the request we shall do all that lies in our power [although we are unable to provide much assistance] as the Americans have lain much upon us, and of late the British have plundered and entirely broke up many amongst us . . . but notwithstanding all this, we are determined by the assistance of Providence, while we have anything amongst us that the distressed both at the Court House and here shall be part of it with us. As we have not made distinctions as to party and their causes [it is the] duty of true Christians at all times to assist the distressed.[51]

Further research might uncover additional examples of public health regulations, the actions of state legislatures and councils of safety, the amount of Loyalist property confiscated, and the medical aspects of martial law. As we have seen, some civilians responded to the presence of incapacitated troops with fear of pestilence, revenge on the Tories, or even sheer indifference to suffering. However, the typical reaction to sick and wounded soldiers during the American Revolution appears to have been compassionate and humanitarian.

[51]Cited in Dorothy Thorne, "North Carolina Friends and the Revolution," *North Carolina Historical Review* 38 (1961): 338.

A Society and
Its War

CHARLES ROYSTER

In the past ten years, historians of the American Revolution have shown a growing interest in the study of the revolutionary war as a crucial part of the study of the era. In publications this interest has taken diverse forms: analyses of army recruitment and supply; examinations of political and religious thought concerning the war; descriptions of the war's effect on communities; interpretations of the war's impact on large segments of society—women, Loyalists, slaves, or opponents of the dominant American political leaders; and, of course, biographies. Although the methods and conclusions of these studies vary widely, they seem to agree that the nature of the war was influenced by the society that was engaged in it. The war, in turn, shaped the revolution of which it was an essential element.

We can now see more clearly that the fighting of the revolutionary war affected many Americans besides those who did the killing and sustained the casualties. The many manifestations of this reciprocal relationship between an army and a people are some of the principal concerns of those who study war and society. Of course, the fruitfulness of this field of inquiry does not depend on a warring society's having the elections, newspapers, voluntary recruits, or legislated taxation and conscription that have been characteristic of

America's national wars. Scholars of Mediterranean antiquity, of medieval Europe, and of North American Indians—to name only a few broad fields—have long emphasized the crucial role of warfare in reflecting or shaping the lives and institutions of whole peoples. Now that students of eighteenth-century America have begun to develop this area of study more fully, they confront, among other important problems, the question of how those distinctive institutions of a republic's popular war—first established for Americans by the Revolution—provide connections between a people and their army in combat.

My own work within this complex field has made me especially interested in one aspect of it: what the eighteenth century called the "moral"—and what the twentieth century might call the "psychological"—influence of the fighting. To make worthwhile generalizations one must evaluate a society's attitudes, and attributing a mental state or a moral outlook to a whole people necessarily depends, in part, on inference and speculation. The biographer, writing about one person, can often trace specific, plausible connections between words and deeds as a basis for speculating about their significance. Assessments of a society must be speculative on a large scale. In fact, many descriptions of American society point not to its psychological unity but to its social divisions—economic, ethnic, sexual, political, sectional, religious—sometimes implicitly or directly denying that there existed among people in these categories a community sufficient to justify our speaking of "a" society.

However, the revolutionary war itself provides forceful evidence that an American society, an organized, self-consciously cooperating people—not just a small minority of Americans—did enter it, wage it, win it, and celebrate it. The governmental instruments for financing and fighting a war had so little capacity for systematic coercion that the war fundamentally depended on voluntary support; even the coercive elements of that support were more communal than official. Thus, one of the most important social categories of the revolutionary war years consisted of the large number of men who bore arms—who, despite other divisions among them, experienced for varying lengths of time the clarifying, unifying effect of being part of a group that enemies were trying to kill. In turn, these men could take the field only because many more thousands of Americans encouraged and sometimes obliged them to do so, intermittently but repeatedly, for eight years. The society fighting its war did not lose all of its internal divisions; but it did demonstrate the existence of elements of community—elements whose importance and strength we can infer from the magnitude of the effort and the willingness to persevere despite large numbers of deaths in proportion to population. It is the moral or psychological bonds between this community and the war it waged that I should like to explore. In what ways did the revolutionary war belong to the public? How did they shape it? How did it touch them? To what extent can we see in the American Revolution some indications of how a populace defines a popular war?

Mobilization for the revolutionary war stressed the importance of reciprocal ties between soldiers and noncombatants. Most direct were the family ties through which people at home knew that their relations were running the risks of the field. The defense of the home remained a constant theme both in recruiting Continental soldiers and in sending short-term militia. Civilian encounters with the British army, its German auxiliaries, and its Loyalist militia often lent bloody verification to this revolutionary rhetoric; invasion and civil war spread widely a danger that made some form of military activity common. Less immediate than family ties but also crucial to the continuation of the war was the material link between soldiers and civilians. The army got paid, though often in promises, by grants from the state legislatures and the Continental Congress; recruits received bounties from states, local governments, and individuals; soldiers were supplied through the flawed but extremely widespread procurement efforts of Continental and state officials. The volume of resources expended to sustain eight years of conflict dramatizes the extent to which an entire people sent their forces to fight and repeatedly demonstrated willingness to keep them in the field. The flow of goods and money, erratic though it was, formed another connection—a material manifestation of a moral bond—between civilians and combatants.

During the revolutionary war, especially at its start and its close, Americans at home often avowed their ties to their army's struggle. They argued that their cause sought not just to defend the material interests of its supporters but also to secure a morally superior political order for themselves and their posterity. War would vindicate principle. Such revolutionaries remained suspicious of the discipline and professional exclusiveness of army officers. Many citizens spoke of their regret that victory entailed so much bloodshed. Nevertheless, they envisioned a principled, even symbolic significance in the necessary conflict. They welcomed the battle because victory would accomplish society's purposes by protecting republican self-government. Victory would also inspire later generations to fight again when liberty seemed threatened. Revolutionary combat, then, was preceded and followed by frequent public assertions that on its fortunes rested the aspirations of a people.

In such a war the populace did not leave the guidance of conflict or the definition of war aims solely in the hands of public officials. Revolutionary leaders showed concern for the attitudes of civilians, repeatedly acknowledging that battlefield successes could win more active support for the cause and that independence could not be won without such support. A popular war created channels of influence running between the society and the waging of the war. The American Revolution developed a variety of such channels and enhanced the sophistication of their communication. Before the revolutionary war began, the decades of political mobilization and resistance to British taxation had amplified the means for expressing public sentiment. Committees that became quasi-governmental bodies, militia units that were as much political as military, newspapers full of letters and essays, ministers whose sermons dwelt on public issues, officeholders who managed public affairs while facing elections annually—these men and these institutions, in the hope of shaping events, remained sensitive registers of the constituencies they addressed. The coming of the war and the declaration of independence increased the importance of this communication, because fighting for independence added to the concerns that could be resolved only by winning popular support.

During the years of the most active military operations, 1775–78 and 1780–81, discussion of the war recurred constantly within these channels of communication, and the lessening of that public concern during the middle years, 1778–80, became a major threat to the achievement of independence. In this discussion several themes illustrate the ways in which complex, often distant military operations strongly moved the populace, who then expressed strong opinions about the conduct of the war.

Americans transmitted rumors and reports of battles with great urgency. Errors, exaggerations, even fictions were common; the hunger for news became an incentive to provide stories, whether or not they had any merit. The frequent use of militia auxiliaries with the army gave thousands of families a personal reason for anxiety, as did the march or threatened march of the British army, which at different times appeared in all parts of the thirteen colonies. Moreover, if the enemy won the war, his instruments of power would pervade America. When reports of American defeat spread and, still worse, turned out to be accurate, they several times led to widespread, desperate alarms among civilians. Howe's invasion of New Jersey in 1776, Burgoyne's march through New York in 1777, the Philips-Arnold invasion of Virginia in 1780–81, and Cornwallis's march through the Carolinas all aroused local panics and regional fears. Perhaps the most widespread reaction, expressed throughout the colonies, came in response to the two major American defeats in 1780—the surrender of Charleston, South Carolina, with its defending army, and the destruction of Horatio Gates's army at Camden. These alarms dramatized with intense emotion the popular conviction that the army's fighting directly affected the public. For analytical purposes historians have often drawn a sharp distinction between the political revolution and the revolutionary war—in fact, have usually divorced the two. But the participants could not safely do so.

There were inextricable ties between political mobilization, constitutional change, internal division, and the exigencies of fighting and financing combat. The fear of invasion and oppression, manifested in wartime alarms, brought the war home to the public. Rumors, flights, musters, and mourning frequently reminded large numbers of Americans that they ran great risks in seeking independence, risks that forced civilians to involve themselves in the war.

This involvement exposed the public to the hazards of war; it also gave them greater responsibility for the conduct of the war. They did not leave it to the generals, but vehemently expressed opinions about the generals' behavior. In the popular version of the war, commanders were more than military professionals. They also seemed to embody qualities of character important to the Revolution, and the public sat in judgment on their success in representing the moral dimensions of the cause. Of course, people wanted generals to be courageous and victorious. These qualifications, however, were supposed to transcend the individual and shape the moral attributes of the war: a general should inspire the liberty-loving courage of citizen volunteers without resorting primarily to traditional hierarchy, coercion, and drill; a general should seek decisive combat quickly, using the powerful advantage of his popular cause rather than unnecessarily prolonging the conflict with obscure, intricate strategic maneuvers. The general, then, was the link between the people and their army. They could not command it, but they could insist that its commander accomplish their goals, moral as well as military. This cast of mind could pillory generals for failure to win, no matter what the army's situation in the field; or, in adversity, it could vest in the general a temporary dictatorship, giving him the people's authority so that he could use his special abilities to save them. In the rise and fall of Generals Charles Lee and Horatio Gates, in the praise and condemnation of Benedict Arnold, in the commemoration of the martyred Joseph Warren and Richard Montgomery, in the unique stature of Washington, the generals served symbolic purposes, whether they wanted to do so or not. Their glory or ruin measured their standing as exemplars of public spirit in a war whose nature the populace, not just the generals, would define. Through the effect of this popular scrutiny, even those generals who might have preferred to fight a classic war of professional armies on limited battlefields became channels of influence through which the public made the war their own.

Crucial to this understanding of the war was the moral significance the revolutionaries saw in combat. The war with Britain would not be a clash of mercenary professionals trying to augment the power and wealth of the state that employed them. Rather, fighting would give Americans the occasion to prove that a popular war exemplified a people's character. A willingness to sacrifice lives, to make war by putting citizens in the ranks, demonstrated a national vigilance in defense of liberty. The assertion of this intrinsic American virtue permeated public praise of American war making. The revolutionaries would win because they were morally superior to their opponents; they would show this superiority by fighting more skillfully, for a nobler cause, with a more persistent dedication. Wartime behavior often did not match these claims. Even so, the claims remained the central justification for the war effort: they were a bond through which colonial rebels could transform themselves into a distinct people with an independent destiny, attained through combat.

Considered in this light, as an effort to vindicate national moral character, the revolutionary war looks like not simply a popular war but even a necessary one—an essential prerequisite for the unity of the new nation, a violent incentive for cohesion in belief and action that no declaration of independence alone could have matched in urgency. In fact, fighting preceded and helped to justify the declaration, rather than the other way around. Thus, in the call for a popular national war we find a recurring stress on the moral benefits of bloodshed, as well as a reiterated demand for the climactic battle that would, by its very destructiveness, prove the national strength and secure the country's existence. Whether or not the war had to occur, once it had begun Americans wanted it to be decisive in the magnitude of sacrifice and in the finality of victory.

Many of the attributes of popular war that are readily recognizable in the American Civil War appeared earlier, in less pronounced form, during the American Revolution. Among these, none is more important than a populace that derived moral exaltation from bloodshed in a virtuous cause, accompanied, as this feeling often was, by the anticipation of a great battle. Creating a citizen army of volunteers and legislatively conscripted civilians made it possible to sustain heavy casualties and yet replace them on a scale that monarchs employing career soldiers could ill afford. In their willingness, even eagerness, to make such sacrifices, Americans claimed to experience a national triumph of principled courage over selfishness. They mourned casualties; they deplored defeats; nevertheless, they rebuilt armies, found new generals, and continued to demand decisive battle. Popular war was bloody war partly because the populace celebrated bloodshed and made it possible for bloodshed to continue.

These broad categories of communication between army and people show some of the ways in which those ties shape the conduct of the war. At the same time, such civilian involvement in the war heightened the impact of the fighting on society. Although American revolutionaries might long remain distant from combat, they were not timeless peasants dispassionately witnessing the struggle of dynasties. They were partisans who expected the war to bring them a better world. At the very least, it brought them a different one. Of course, war, popular or not, can have profound effects on the societies it touches. Casualties, taxes, governmental expenditures, physical destruction, political upheaval—any or all of these can leave a society much changed in ways that the war makers may never have intended. However, a popular war undertaken to serve a public purpose carries with it a conscious intention to use war as an instrument. And this intent implies a corresponding burden of responsibility. The American revolutionaries linked their moral vision to the army's combat, but in doing so they made that moral outlook susceptible to the psychological effects of violence. This reciprocal effect of war is less easily measured than casualties, taxes, and physical damage. Yet it may be closely tied to them, and it may perpetuate their psychological influence long after the material costs have been liquidated.

A war may originate in disagreements over legislation, constitutions, alliances, or territories. In the popular wars—the Revolution and the Civil War—other public concerns less susceptible to negotiation and compromise sought expression through combat. Victory seemed to promise not just independence or political union or newly delineated borders—those specific, measurable achievements—but it seemed also to offer the public a resolution of peacetime moral concerns.

American revolutionaries constantly claimed that they were demonstrating the ability of the people's virtue to defend liberty against a corrupt tyrant. The survival of this virtuous devotion to liberty, the long-term ability of the people to govern themselves, had no guarantee. Many Americans worried that devotion might not be strong enough. The revolutionary war and, on a larger scale, the Civil War came almost as a relief to those who had seen reason to doubt their country's moral strength. These doubters feared that self-government might be lost due to internal divisions. Such divisions took diverse forms: conflicts among sections, factions, or groups with divergent economic interests; disagreements in party loyalty or religion; and, most frightening of all, underlying many sources of conflict, a selfishness that in its isolation and materialism would destroy people's capacity to unite altruistically in the service of ideals. Against these threats, principled warfare seemed to prove the public solidarity and idealism.

Along these lines, the Continental army and the revolutionary militia were supposed to promote cooperation among Americans of different sections, political views, or social status. Orators constantly celebrated the heroism of citizens in all stations of life who gathered to risk their lives in the cause. This vision did not last long in practice, but it expressed a widely shared conception of the significance of the fighting: the war would, through its urgent defense of all people's welfare, dramatize their underlying unity. When that unity eroded in the wartime adversity of defeat, betrayal, and profiteering, the army's final victories and the winning of independence became the occasions for repeated assertions that the vision of 1775 still prevailed. A people's willingness to withstand horrible bloodshed stood as climactic proof of disinterested idealism.

In Britain during the Crimean War and again in America during the Civil War, the very popularity of the conflicts seemed to vindicate going to war, inasmuch as the public's readiness to accept casualties demonstrated that the nation had not surrendered its idealistic spirit to the materialism of a commercial age. In this formulation of popular war, the crucial link between the citizens and their army did not lie in the size of the army or the representativeness of the army as a cross-section of the population. The very different armies of 1776, 1854, and 1865 were "popular" insofar as their activities held moral meaning for the societies that mobilized them. The American revolutionaries made their war a psychological as well as physical test of their ability to endure as a republic. It was to be a measure of principle no less than of resources. The Civil War generation posed this challenge again on an even more profound, complex, and costly scale. However, in merging ideals with warfare, these societies also ran a risk—not just that they might lose but also that the fighting might grow so awesome, so overwhelming, that the ideals it supposedly served would lapse into the background or be lost.

Today, many people are immediately skeptical of the notion of a morally inspiring war. To compare uplifting wartime rhetoric with the conduct of armies in combat is to see a frequent, troubling disparity. Intelligible goals and glorious self-sacrifice seem to give way to meaningless violence among opposing armies and against noncombatants. We have learned to expect this disillusionment.

From Stephen Crane's *The Red Badge of Courage* to Paul Fussell's *The Great War and Modern Memory*, writers have reiterated this ironic contrast between the noble call to arms and the chaotic destructiveness of antlike armies. This irony has become the predominant theme in the literature of America's war in Vietnam. We are no longer surprised to learn that war is hell or that, in the words of Michael Herr, "hell sucks." Indeed, many of us have become so familiar with the outlook of modern literature on war that we find it hard to believe that combat can be analyzed through the intentions of its supporters or that those intentions partook of idealism not only in starting the war but also in pursuing its destructive course.

And yet, in the lines of influence between society and combat that are characteristic of popular war, there may be an intelligible connection between the inspiring moral appeal and the shocking violence. Whether or not battles took the shape that generals wanted, whether or not war accomplished the purposes that officials proclaimed, the war may still have carried out society's moral purposes. Through supporting and celebrating combat, a people could establish in an elemental way their commitment to the principles that they claimed as the basis of their unity.

By this reasoning, the destructiveness of the war—far from refuting the participants' claims to be idealistic—was partly a consequence of that idealism, a consequence that was made possible because the war was a popular war and the people wanted destructiveness. Consider, for example, the burning of Columbia, South Carolina, by Sherman's army on the night of February 17, 1865. Here is an event that looks made to order for the modern literary view of war—thousands of drunken soldiers, abetted by newly freed slaves, running uncontrolled through a city filled with women, children, and old men; robbing, plundering, and assaulting; setting fires that heavy winds blew into a firestorm that consumed a large part of the city, leading to deaths by fire, shock, and exposure. One could interpret this scene as the meaningless, anarchic violence of uncontrollable men; one could see in it the advent of modernity, that ill-defined phenomenon in which vast destructive forces seem to overpower individual intent; or, like the Southerners, one could attribute it to the depravity of William Tecumseh Sherman. However, many Union soldiers said explicitly that they had acted intentionally. According to their account of the fire, South Carolina and especially Columbia got what they deserved for leading the cause of secession, arrogating to the state the superiority of a slaveholding society over a free one, and thereby provoking the Civil War. Although few historians would regard the Union soldiers' interpretation as complete, it was a popular outlook in Northern states, where many people had advocated devastation of the South. The burning of Columbia did not have official approval as governmental policy, but it reflected a widely shared view of the causes of the war and the importance of winning. One could interpret this seemingly anarchic scene of destruction as a direct, predictable consequence of whole societies' setting out to resolve fundamental public issues by fighting each other.

When an entire society goes to war, the very scale of moral and material commitment can make the war more awesome and, ultimately, shocking. How does the society deal with these disturbing results of its own decisions? One of the most common responses to this problem has been to evade it—to celebrate the outcome of the war as justification for the public's willingness to undertake it, while attributing the worst excesses to some cause for which the public is not responsible. In the United States, the revolutionary war and the War of 1812 established this reassuring interpretative pattern in which wartime and postwar hyperbole and sentimentality revived the original vision of an easy, glorious, romantic war, muting the memory of lapses into popular lethargy, selfish corruption, or chaotic violence. The legend did not deny that adversity and destruction had occurred; in fact, it celebrated them. But it made them purposeful, necessary, and heroic, or omitted them from the list of the people's accomplishments, thus excluding such excesses from any connection with popular ideals.

The revolutionary war outlined channels of popular support for war and public participation in it. The Revolution also established the patriotic precedent of fighting a heroic war over fundamental issues. The vision of the revolutionaries recurred often in the literature of the Civil War, in private letters as well as in speeches, just as the moral inspiration of the Civil War recurred in the rhetoric of the Spanish-American War. The armies were supposed to exemplify societal ideals. They were not mercenaries serving temporary national interests; they came from the citizenry to defend the nation's existence. And war for the nation's existence, the principal rationale for modern war, obviously must be necessary and all of its methods justified.

Popular war, no matter what its official goals, ultimately becomes, like the American Revolution, war for the nation's survival, in the eyes of its advocates. They may refer to territorial rights, to political institutions, or to moral principles. Arguments that make any or all of these the basis for the nation's safety inevitably set the stakes of war very high. The more fully the American revolutionaries or the Civil War generation or other creators and defenders of nationhood incorporate a citizen army, public involvement, and a body of ideals into their war, the less tolerable is defeat—and, therefore, the more justifiable drastic war measures seem. William Tecumseh Sherman acknowledged that in peacetime the voters and their elected officials ruled the nation through law and reason. But when voters and their leaders could not maintain the law or the nation peaceably, and so resorted to war, they forfeited the protection of logic and peacetime precedents. Then they entered the world of force, which knows no necessary, logical restraints, though its wielders try to restrain it for reasons of state. Sherman said, in effect, that those who were appalled by the bloodshed and devastation of the Civil War ought to have avoided war. Or, if war seemed inevitable and necessary, they ought to know that they, not just he, had created it in all its aspects.

If the American Revolution, considered as a popular war, has meaning that goes beyond its own period, one element of such meaning is that a republic cannot disown its war, even when the fighting looks appalling rather than inspiring. Shakespeare could allow King Henry V to tell a soldier that the responsibility for the morally troubling violence rested on the king's head alone. But the American Revolution explicitly deprived citizens and soldiers of this opportunity for moral abdication by asserting that the founding and survival of the nation were a public responsibility. The central element of popular war is this appeal to fundamentals—in ideals, in participation, and in methods. Because it originates in fundamental premises and because it implicitly sanctions extreme measures, we may, if we look at such war closely, shrink from seeing America reflected in all American wars. Yet only by looking closely can we address the problems inherent in a republican government's resort to force on behalf of popular ideals. Americans have often heard from Jefferson, Lincoln, Wilson, and others that their wars preserve for other peoples the hope of liberty and self-government. Whatever one's assessment of this interpretation, one can conclude that the popular war for nationhood—the necessary, ideological, drastic conflict—is among the most enduring examples that the United States has offered the world.

Contributors

LAWRENCE E. BABITS completed his Ph.D. in anthropology at Brown University and is now teaching in the Department of History at Armstrong State College, Savannah, Georgia. He is active in living history and has been a member since 1967 of the re-created First Maryland Regiment.

DOUGLAS CLARK BAXTER, Associate Professor of History at Ohio University, published his study of *Servants of the Sword: French Intendants of the Army, 1630–1670*, in 1976.

DANIEL J. BEATTIE earned his Ph.D. at Duke University and is presently finishing a biography of Jeffery Lord Amherst.

RICHARD L. BLANCO is Professor of History at the State University of New York, College at Brockport. His published works include: *Wellington's Surgeon General: Sir James McGrigor* (1974), *Physician of the American Revolution: Jonathan Potts* (1979), *Rommel the Desert Warrior* (1982), and a select annotated bibliography, *The War of the American Revolution* (1984).

ROBIN F. A. FABEL is Associate Professor of History at Auburn University and is a specialist in colonial America.

DOUGLAS E. LEACH is Professor of History at Vanderbilt University. He is the author of many works on warfare in early America, including: *Flintlock and Tomahawk: New England in King Philip's War* (1958), *The Northern Colonial Frontier, 1607–1763* (1966), and *Arms for Empire: A Military History of the British Colonies in North America, 1607–1763* (1973).

JOHN R. MCNEILL took his doctoral degree in history at Duke University and now teaches at Goucher College in Maryland. He has recently been working on an ecological history of Brazil and on the transformation of peasant communities in Mediterranean Europe since 1870. His book, *Havana, Louisbourg, and the Atlantic World, 1700–1763*, has been published by the University of North Carolina Press.

CHARLES ROYSTER wrote the prize-winning work *A Revolutionary People at War: The Continental Army and American Character, 1775–1783* (1979). His second book, *Light-Horse Harry Lee and the Legacy of the American Revolution* (1981), also won critical acclaim. In 1982–83 he held a Guggenheim Fellowship; he has since returned to his teaching post at Louisiana State University and is currently working on a book about the Civil War era.

SHEILA L. SKEMP earned her Ph.D. at the University of Iowa. She was coeditor of *Foundations of American Nationalism* (1978) and now teaches at the University of Mississippi.

CLAUDE C. STURGILL is Professor of History at the University of Florida. His books on the French army and administration include: *Marshal Villars in the War of the Spanish Succession* (1965), *Claude le Blanc: Civil Servant of the King* (1976), *La Formation de la Milice Permanente en France, 1726–1730* (1977), *L'Organisation et l'Administration de la Justice Prévôtale, 1720–1730* (1980), and *Le Financement de l'Armée de Louis XV: Les Opérations de Commissaires de Guerres, 1715–1730* (1985). The essay in this volume will eventually become part of a book-length study: "Money for the Bourbon Army: The Budget of the Secretary of State at War, 1720–1790."

MAARTEN ULTEE, Associate Professor of History at The University of Alabama, published *The Abbey of St. Germain des Prés in the Seventeenth Century* in 1981. He is continuing research on social mobility and international scholarly communication in early modern Europe.

Index

190

16B⅟₂